THE APARTMENT AND
THE FORTUNE COOKIE

series edited and designed by Ian Cameron

THE APARTMENT

and

THE FORTUNE

COOKIE

two screenplays by Billy Wilder

and I.A.L. Diamond

STUDIO VISTA

Produced by November Books Limited for Movie Magazine Limited, 23-29 Emerald Street, London, WC1N 3QL.

Published by Studio Vista Limited, Blue Star House, Highgate Hill, London, N19.

Text set by Yendall & Company Limited, Riscatype House, 22-25 Red Lion Court, Fleet Street, London, EC4.

Printed by Compton Printing Limited, Pembroke Road, Stocklake, Aylesbury, Bucks.

Bound by Dorstel Press Limited, West Road, Templefields, Harlow, Essex.

Printed in England.

This edition is not for sale in the United States or Canada.

SBN 289.70067.1 (paperback)
     289.70068.x (hardback)

Stills by Courtesy of United Artists and The Mirisch Corporation.

Our thanks are due, above all, to Messrs Wilder and Diamond for their permission to publish these two screenplays. We also wish to thank Mark Shivas for providing the initial impetus for the production of this volume and Charles Berman of United Artists in London for lending us copies of the films.

Frontispiece: Billy Wilder and I. A. L. Diamond in Britain for the shooting of The Private Life of Sherlock Holmes.

This volume contains the two original screenplays (as opposed to adaptations) so far written by Billy Wilder and I. A. L. Diamond. It is worth pointing out that we are publishing the screenplays as written by Wilder and Diamond rather than a description reconstituted from the films themselves, as that treatment would have produced no more than an inadequate substitute for the films themselves and would have lost the economy of the original writing among the minutiae of documentation. Instead we have a record of the details of dress and décor which the authors themselves thought to be important and of the screenplay's verbal impressions (like the opening of *The Fortune Cookie*) which Wilder has translated into visuals.

Inevitably, the screenplays do not exactly correspond with the final versions of the films, though the changes are mainly very minor. In particular, *The Fortune Cookie* hardly departs from the screenplay at all: a tiny scene (117) seems to have been dropped, and two of the chapter titles have been changed – Chapter 9 from 'The Whirlpool' to 'The Goldfish Bowl' and Chapter 14 from 'The Gravy Train' to 'The Taste of Money'. The one notable addition after the screenplay is in Sandy's comment about Willie Gingrich in scene 88 which, in the film, has the line: 'He could find a loophole in the Ten Commandments.'

The Apartment has been modified slightly more between screenplay and release. The opening shot of a computer keyboard has been replaced by an aerial shot of New York, and there have been quite a number of minor cuts made in the editing to tighten up the first quarter of the film. The dialogue delivered in the film quite often slightly paraphrases the screenplay version.

Our thanks are due, first of all, to Messrs Wilder and Diamond for their permission to publish these screenplays. We also wish to thank Charles Berman of United Artists for lending us copies of the films. Stills are by courtesy of United Artists and the Mirisch Company.

The illustrations are taken from production stills and therefore do not correspond exactly to the camera set-ups.

THE
APARTMENT

Produced and directed by Billy Wilder
Written by Billy Wilder and I. A. L. Diamond
Associate Producers: I. A. L. Diamond and Doane Harrison
Director of Photography: Joseph La Shelle A.S.C.
Photographed in Panavision (black and white)
Art Director: Alexander Trauner
Set Decorator: Edward G. Boyle
Film Editor: Daniel Mandell A.C.E.
Sound: Fred Lau
Music Editor: Sid Sidney

Sound effects Editor: Del Harris
Production Manager: Allen K. Wood
Assistant Director: Hal Polaire
Properties: Tom Plews
Script continuity: May Wale
Special effects: Milt Rice
Make-up: Harry Ray S.M.A.
Copyright MCMLX by the Mirisch Company Inc.
Length: 125 minutes
U.K. Censor Certificate: A
Distributed by United Artists

C. C. (Bud) Baxter	JACK LEMMON	Karl Matuschka	JOHNNY SEVEN
Fran Kubelik	SHIRLEY MACLAINE	Mrs Dreyfuss	NAOMI STEVENS
J. D. Sheldrake	FRED MACMURRAY	Mrs Lieberman	FRANCES WEINTRAUB LAX
Mr Dobisch	RAY WALSTON	The Blonde	JOYCE JAMESON
Mr Kirkeby	DAVID LEWIS	Mr Vanderhof	WILLARD WATERMAN
Dr Dreyfuss	JACK KRUSCHEN	Mr Eichelberger	DAVID WHITE
Sylvia	JOAN SHAWLEE	The Bartender	BENNY BURT
Miss Olsen	EDIE ADAMS	The Santa Claus	HAL SMITH
Margie MacDougall	HOPE HOLIDAY		

1 A DESK COMPUTER

A man's hand is punching out a series of figures on the keyboard.

BUD'S VOICE

On November first, 1959, the population of New York City was 8,042,783. If you laid all these people end to end, figuring an average height of five feet six and a half inches, they would reach from Times Square to the outskirts of Karachi, Pakistan. I know facts like this because I work for an insurance company –

2 THE INSURANCE BUILDING – A WET, FALL DAY

It's a big mother, covering a square block in lower Manhattan, all glass and aluminum, jutting into the leaden sky.

– Consolidated Life of New York. We are one of the top five companies in the country – last year we wrote nine-point-three billion dollars worth of policies. Our home office has 31,259 employees – which is more than the entire population of Natchez, Mississippi, or Gallup, New Mexico.

3 INT. NINETEENTH FLOOR

Acres of gray steel desks, gray steel filing cabinets, and steel-gray faces under indirect light. One wall is lined with glass-enclosed cubicles for the supervisory personnel. It is all very neat, antiseptic, impersonal. The only human touch is supplied by a bank of IBM machines, clacking away cheerfully in the background.

I work on the nineteenth floor – Ordinary Policy Department – Premium Accounting Division – Section W – desk number 861.

4 DESK 861

Like every other desk, it has a small name plate attached to the side. This one reads C. C. BAXTER. BAXTER is about thirty, serious, hardworking, unobtrusive. He wears a Brooks Brothers type suit, which he bought somewhere on Seventh Avenue, upstairs. There is a stack of perforated premium cards in front of him, and he is totaling them on the computing machine. He looks off.

My name is C. C. Baxter – C. for Calvin, C. for Clifford – however, most people call me Bud. I've been with Consolidated Life for three years and ten months. I started in the branch office in Cincinnati, then transferred to New York. My take-home pay is $94.70 a week, and there are the usual fringe benefits.

5 ELECTRIC WALL CLOCK

It shows 5:19. With a click, the minute hand jumps to 5:20, and a piercing bell goes off.

The hours in our department are 8:50 to 5:20 –

13

6 FULL SHOT – OFFICE

Instantly all work stops. Papers are being put away, typewriters and computing machines are covered, and everybody starts clearing out. Within ten seconds, the place is empty – except for Bud Baxter, still bent over his work, marooned in a sea of abandoned desks.

– they're staggered by floors, so that sixteen elevators can handle the 31,259 employees without a serious traffic jam. As for myself, I very often stay on at the office and work for an extra hour or two – especially when the weather is bad. It's not that I'm overly ambitious – it's just a way of killing time, until it's all right for me to go home. You see, I have this little problem with my apartment –

DISSOLVE TO:

7 STREET IN THE WEST SIXTIES – EVENING

Bud, wearing a weather-beaten Ivy League raincoat and a narrow-brimmed brown hat, comes walking slowly down the street skirting the puddles on the sidewalk. He stops in front of a converted brownstone, looks up. The windows on the second floor are lit, but the shades are drawn. From inside drifts the sound of cha cha music.

I live in the West Sixties – just half a block from Central Park. My rent is $84 a month. It used to be eighty until last July when Mrs. Lieberman, the landlady, put in a second-hand air conditioning unit. It's a real nice apartment – nothing fancy – but kind of cozy – just right for a bachelor. The only problem is – I can't always get in when I want to.

8 INT. THE APARTMENT – EVENING

What used to be the upstairs parlor of a one-family house in the early 1900's has been chopped up into living room, bedroom, bathroom and kitchen. The wallpaper is faded, the carpets are threadbare, and the upholstered furniture could stand shampooing. There are lots of books, a record player, stacks of records, a television set (21 inches and 24 payments), unframed prints from the Museum of Modern Art (Picasso, Braque, Klee) tacked up on the walls.

Only one lamp is lit, for mood, and a cha cha record is spinning around on the phonograph. On the coffee table in front of the couch are a couple of cocktail glasses, a pitcher with some martini dregs, an almost empty bottle of vodka, a soup bowl with a few melting ice cubes at the bottom, some potato chips, an ashtray filled with cigar stubs and lipstick-stained cigarette butts, and a woman's handbag.

MR. KIRKEBY, a dapper, middle-aged man, stands in front of the mirror above the fake fireplace, buttoning up his vest. He does not notice that the buttons are out of alignment.

KIRKEBY (*calling off*): Come on, Sylvia. It's getting late.

SYLVIA, a first baseman of a dame, redheaded and saftig, comes cha cha-ing into the room, trying to fasten a necklace as she hums along with the music. She dances amorously up to Kirkeby.

KIRKEBY: Cut it out, Sylvia. We got to get out of here.

He helps her with the necklace, then turns off the phonograph.

SYLVIA: What's the panic? I'm going to have another martooni.

She crosses to the coffee table, starts to pour the remnants of the vodka into the pitcher.

KIRKEBY: Please, Sylvia! It's a quarter to nine!

SYLVIA (*dropping slivers of ice into the pitcher*): First you can't wait to get me up here, and now – rush, rush, rush! Makes a person feel cheap.

KIRKEBY: Sylvia – sweetie – it's not that – but I promised the guy I'd be out of here by eight o'clock, positively.

SYLVIA (*pouring martini*): What guy? Whose apartment is this, anyway?

KIRKEBY (*exasperated*): What's the difference? Some schnook that works in the office.

9 EXT. BROWNSTONE HOUSE – EVENING

Bud is pacing back and forth, throwing an occasional glance at the lit windows of his apartment. A middle-aged woman with a dog on a leash approaches along the sidewalk. She is MRS. LIEBERMAN, the dog is a Scottie, and they are both wearing raincoats. Seeing them, Bud leans casually against the stoop.

MRS. LIEBERMAN: Good evening, Mr. Baxter.

BUD: Good evening, Mrs. Lieberman.

MRS. LIEBERMAN: Some weather we're having. Must be from all the meshugass at Cape Canaveral. (*she is half-way up the steps*) You locked out of your apartment?

BUD: No, no. Just waiting for a friend. Good night, Mrs. Lieberman.

MRS. LIEBERMAN: Good night, Mr. Baxter.

She and the Scottie disappear into the house. Bud resumes pacing, his eyes on the apartment windows. Suddenly he stops – the lights have gone out.

10 INT. SECOND FLOOR LANDING – EVENING

Kirkeby, in coat and hat, stands in the open doorway of the darkened apartment.

KIRKEBY: Come on – come on, Sylvia!

Sylvia comes cha cha-ing out, wearing an imitation Persian lamb coat, her hat askew on her head, bag, gloves and an umbrella in her hand.

SYLVIA: Some setup you got here. A real, honest-to-goodness love nest.

KIRKEBY: Ssssssh.

He locks the door, slips the key under the doormat.

SYLVIA (*still cha cha-ing*): You're one button off, Mr. Kirkeby

She points to his exposed vest. Kirkeby looks down, sees that the buttons are out of line. He starts to rebutton them as they move down the narrow, dimly-lit stairs.

SYLVIA: You got to watch those things. Wives are getting smarter all the time. Take Mr. Bernheim – in the Claims Department – came home one night with lipstick on his shirt – told his wife he had a shrimp cocktail for lunch – so she took it out to the lab and had it analyzed –

so now she has the house in Great Neck and the children and the new Jaguar –
KIRKEBY: Don't you ever stop talking?

11 EXT. BROWNSTONE HOUSE – EVENING

Bud, standing on the sidewalk, sees the front door start to open. He moves quickly into the areaway, almost bumping into the ashcans, stands in the shadow of the stoop with his back turned discreetly

toward Kirkeby and Sylvia as they come down the steps.

KIRKEBY: Where do you live?

SYLVIA: I told you – with my mother.

KIRKEBY: Where does *she* live?

SYLVIA: A hundred and seventy-ninth street – the Bronx.

KIRKEBY: All right – I'll take you to the subway.

SYLVIA: Like hell you will. You'll buy me a cab.

KIRKEBY: Why do all you dames have to live in the Bronx?

SYLVIA: You mean you bring other girls up here?

KIRKEBY: Certainly not. I'm a happily married man.

They move down the street. Bud appears from the areaway, glances after them, then mounts the steps, goes through the front door.

12   INT. VESTIBULE – EVENING

There are eight mailboxes. Bud opens his, takes out a magazine in a paper wrapper and a few letters, proceeds up the staircase.

13   INT. SECOND FLOOR LANDING – EVENING

Bud, glancing through his mail, comes up to the door of his apartment. As he bends down to lift the

doormat, the door of the rear apartment opens and MRS. DREYFUSS, *a jovial well-fed middle-aged woman, puts out a receptacle full of old papers and empty cans. Bud looks around from his bent position.*

BUD: Oh. Hello there, Mrs. Dreyfuss.

MRS. DREYFUSS: Something the matter?

BUD: I seem to have dropped my key. (*faking a little search*)

Oh – here it is.

He slides it out from under the mat, straightens up.

MRS. DREYFUSS: Such a racket I heard in your place – maybe you had burglars.

BUD: Oh, you don't have to worry about that – nothing in there that anybody would want to steal . . . (*unlocking door quickly*) Good night, Mrs. Dreyfuss.

He ducks into the apartment.

14   INT. APARTMENT – EVENING

Bud snaps on the lights, drops the mail and the key on a small table, looks around with distaste at the mess his visitors have left behind. He sniffs the stale air, crosses to the window, pulls up the shade, opens it wide. Now he takes off his hat and raincoat, gathers up the remains of the cocktail party from the coffee table. Loaded down with glasses, pitcher, empty vodka bottle, ice bowl and potato chips, he starts toward the kitchen.

The doorbell rings. Bud stops, undecided what to do with the stuff in his hands, then crosses to the hall door, barely manages to get it open. Mr. Kirkeby barges in past him.

KIRKEBY: The little lady forgot her galoshes.

He scours the room for the missing galoshes.

BUD: Mr. Kirkeby, I don't like to complain – but you were supposed to be out of here by eight.

KIRKEBY: I know, Buddy-boy, I know. But those things don't always run on schedule – like a Greyhound bus.

BUD: I don't mind in the summer – but on a rainy night – and I haven't had any dinner yet –

KIRKEBY: Sure, sure. Look, kid – I put in a good word for you with Sheldrake, in Personnel.

BUD (*perking up*): Mr. Sheldrake?

KIRKEBY: That's right. We were discussing our department – manpower-wise – and promotion-wise – (*finds the galoshes behind a chair*) – and I told him what a bright boy you were. They're always on the lookout for young executives.

BUD: Thank you, Mr. Kirkeby.

KIRKEBY (*starting toward door*): You're on your way up, Buddy-boy. And you're practically out of liquor.

BUD: I know. Mr. Eichelberger – in the Mortgage Loan Department – last night he had a little Halloween party here –

KIRKEBY: Well, lay in some vodka and some vermouth – and put my name on it.

BUD: Yes, Mr. Kirkeby. You still owe me for the last two bottles –

KIRKEBY: I'll pay you on Friday. (*in the open doorway*) And whatever happened to those little cheese crackers you used to have around?

He exits, shutting the door.

BUD (*making a mental note*): Cheese crackers.

He carries his load into the kitchen.

The kitchen is minute and cluttered. On the drainboard are an empty vermouth bottle, some ice-cube trays, a jar with one olive in it, and a crumpled potato-chip bag.

Bud comes in, dumps his load on the drainboard, opens the old-fashioned refrigerator. He takes out a frozen chicken dinner, turns the oven on, lights it with a match, rips the protective paper off the aluminium tray and shoves it in.

Now he starts to clean up the mess on the drainboard. He rinses the cocktail glasses, is about to empty the martini pitcher into the sink, thinks better of it. He pours the contents into a glass, plops the lone olive out of the jar, scoops up the last handful of potato chips, toasts an imaginary companion, and drinks up. Then he pulls a wastebasket from under the sink. It is brimful of liquor bottles, and Bud adds the empty vodka and vermouth bottles and the olive jar. Picking up the heavy receptacle, he carries it through the living room toward the hall door.

15 INT. SECOND FLOOR LANDING – EVENING

The door of Bud's apartment opens, and Bud comes out with the wastebasket full of empty bottles. Just then, DR. DAVID DREYFUSS, whose wife we met earlier, comes trudging up the stairs. He is a tall, heavy-set man of fifty, with a bushy mustache, wearing a bulky overcoat and carrying an aged medical bag.

DR. DREYFUSS: Good evening, Baxter.

BUD: Hi, Doc, Had a late call?

DR. DREYFUSS: Yeah. Some clown at Schrafft's 57th Street ate a club sandwich, and forgot to take out the toothpick.

BUD: Oh. *(sets down wastebasket)* 'Bye, Doc.

DR. DREYFUSS *(indicating bottles)*: Say, Baxter – the way you're belting that stuff, you must have a pair of cast-iron kidneys.

BUD: Oh, that's not me. It's just that once in a while, I have some people in for a drink.

DR. DREYFUSS: As a matter of fact, you must be an iron man all around. From what I hear through the walls, you got something going for you every night.

BUD: I'm sorry if it gets noisy –

DR. DREYFUSS: Sometimes, there's a twi-night double-header. *(shaking his head)* A nebbish like you!

BUD *(uncomfortable)*: Yeah. Well – see you, Doc. *(starts to back through door)*

DR. DREYFUSS: You know, Baxter – I'm doing some research at the Columbia Medical Center – and I wonder if you could do us a favor?

BUD: Me?

DR. DREYFUSS: When you make out your will – and the way you're going, you should – would you mind leaving your body to the University?

BUD: My body? I'm afraid you guys would be

disappointed. Good night, Doc.

DR. DREYFUSS: Slow down, kid.

He starts into the rear apartment as Bud closes the door.

16   INT. APARTMENT – EVENING

Bud, loosening his tie, goes into the kitchen, opens the oven, turns off the gas. He takes a coke out of the refrigerator, uncaps it, gets a knife and fork from a drawer, and using his handkerchief as a potholder, pulls the hot aluminum tray out of the oven. He carries everything out into the living room.

In the living room, Bud sets his dinner down on the coffee table, settles himself on the couch. He rears up as something stabs him, reaches under his buttocks, pulls out a hairpin. He drops it into an ashtray, tackles his dinner. Without even looking, he reaches over to the end table and presses the remote TV station-selector. He takes a sip from the coke bottle, his eyes on the TV screen across the room.

The picture on the TV set jells quickly. Against a background of crisscrossing searchlights, a pompous announcer is making his spiel.

ANNOUNCER: – from the world's greatest library of film classics, we proudly present – (*fanfare*) Greta Garbo – John Barrymore – Joan Crawford – Wallace Beery – and Lionel Barrymore in – (*fanfare*) GRAND HOTEL!

There is an extended fanfare. Bud leans forward, chewing excitedly on a chicken leg.

ANNOUNCER: But first, a word from our sponsor. If you smoke the modern way, don't be fooled by phony filter claims –

Bud, still eating, automatically reaches for the station-selector, pushes the button.

A new channel pops on. It features a Western – Cockamamie Indians are attacking a stagecoach. That's not for Bud. He switches to another station. In a frontier saloon, Gower Street cowboys are dismantling the furniture and each other.

Bud wearily changes channels. But he can't get

away from Westerns – on this station, the U.S. Cavalry is riding to the rescue. Will they get there in time?

Bud doesn't wait to find out. He switches channels again, and is back where he started.

On the screen, once more, is the announcer standing in front of the crisscrossing searchlights.

ANNOUNCER: And now, Grand Hotel – starring Greta Garbo, John Barrymore, Joan Crawford – (*Bud is all eyes and ears again*) – Wallace Beery, and Lionel Barrymore. But first – a word from our *alternate* sponsor. (*unctuously*) Friends, do you have wobbly dentures – ?

That does it. Bud turns the set off in disgust.

The TV screen blacks out, except for a small pinpoint of light in the center, which gradually fades away.

In the bathroom, Bud, in pajamas by now, is brushing his teeth. From the shower rod hang three pairs of socks on stretchers. Bud takes a vial from the medicine shelf, shakes out a sleeping pill, washes it down with a glass of water. He turns the light off, walks into the bedroom.

In the bedroom, the single bed is made, and the lamp on the night table is on. Bud plugs in the electric blanket, turns the dial on. Then he climbs into bed, props up the pillow behind him. From the night table, he picks up the magazine that arrived in the mail, slides it out of the wrapper, opens it. It's the new issue of PLAYBOY. Bud leafs through it till he comes to the pièce de résistance of the magazine. He unfolds the overleaf, glances at it casually, refolds it, then turns to the back of the magazine and starts to read.

What he is so avidly interested in is the men's fashion section. There is a layout titled WHAT THE YOUNG EXECUTIVE WILL WEAR. *with a sub-head reading, The Bowler is Back. Illustrating the article are several photographs of male models wearing various styles of bowlers.*

Bud is definitely in the market for a bowler, but somehow his mind starts wandering. He turns back to the overleaf again, unfolds it, studies it, then holds the magazine up vertically to get a different perspective on the subject. By now the sleeping pill is beginning to take effect, and he yawns. He drops the magazine on the floor, kills the light, settles down to sleep. The room is dark except for the glow from the dial of the electric blanket.

Three seconds. Then the phone jangles shrilly in the living room. Bud stumbles groggily out of bed, and putting on his slippers, makes his way into the living room. He switches on the light, picks up the phone.

BUD: Hello ? – Hello ? – yes, this is Baxter.

17 INT. PHONE BOOTH IN A MAN-HATTAN BAR – NIGHT

On the phone is a hearty man of about forty-five, nothing but personality, most of it obnoxious. His name is DOBISCH. *Outside the booth is a blonde babe, slightly boozed, and beyond there is a suggestion of the packed, smoky joint.*

DOBISCH: Hiya, Buddy-boy. I'm in this bar on Sixty-first Street – and I got to thinking about you – and I figured I'd give you a little buzz.

18 BUD – ON PHONE

BUD: Well, that's very nice of you – but who is this?

19 INT. PHONE BOOTH

DOBISCH: Dobisch – Joe Dobisch, in Administration.

20 BUD – ON PHONE

BUD (*snapping to attention*): Oh, yes, Mr. Dobisch. I didn't recognize your voice –

21 INT. PHONE BOOTH

DOBISCH: That's okay, Buddy-boy. Now like I was saying, I'm in this joint on Sixty-first – and I think I got lucky – (*glances towards blonde*) – she's a skater with the Ice Show – (*he chuckles*) – and I thought maybe I could bring her up for a quiet drink.

22 BUD – ON PHONE

BUD: I'm sorry, Mr. Dobisch. You know I like to help you guys out – but it's sort of late – so why don't we make it some other time?

23 INT. PHONE BOOTH

DOBISCH: Buddy-boy – she won't keep that long – not even on ice. Listen, kid, I can't pass this up – she looks like Marilyn Monroe.

24 BUD – ON PHONE

BUD: I don't care if it *is* Marilyn Monroe – I'm

already in bed – and I've taken a sleeping pill – so I'm afraid the answer is no.

25 INT. PHONE BOOTH

DOBISCH (*pulling rank*). Look, Baxter – we're making out the monthly efficiency rating – and I'm putting you in the top ten. Now you don't want to louse yourself up, do you?

26 BUD – ON PHONE

BUD: Of course not. But – how can I be efficient in the office if I don't get enough sleep at night?

27 INT. PHONE BOOTH

DOBISCH: It's only eleven – and I just want the place for forty-five minutes.
The blonde opens the door of the phone booth, leans in.
BLONDE: I'm getting lonely. Who are you talking to, anyway?
DOBISCH: My mother.
BLONDE: That's sweet. That's real sweet.
Dobisch shuts the door in her face.
DOBISCH (*into phone again*): Make it thirty minutes. What do you say, Bud?

28 BUD – ON PHONE

BUD (*a last stand*): I'm all out of liquor – and there's no clean glasses – no cheese crackers – no nothing.

29 INT. PHONE BOOTH

DOBISCH: Let me worry about that. Just leave the key under the mat and clear out.

30 INT. APARTMENT

BUD: (*into phone; resigned*): Yes, Mr. Dobisch.
He hangs up, shuffles back into the bedroom.
BUD (*muttering to himself*): Anything you say, Mr. Dobisch – no trouble at all, Mr. Dobisch – be my guest –
He reappears from the bedroom, pulling his trousers on over his pajama pants.

BUD: – We never close at Buddy-boy's – looks like Marilyn Monroe – (*he chuckles à la Dobisch*) *Putting on his raincoat and hat, Bud opens the hall door, takes the key from the table, shoves it under the doormat. His eyes fall on the Dreyfuss apartment, and there is some concern on his face. He picks up a pad and pencil from the table, prints something in block letters. Tearing off the top sheet, he impales it on the spindle of the phonograph, then walks out, closing the door behind him. The note reads:*

NOT TOO LOUD THE NEIGHBORS ARE COMPLAINING

31 EXT. BROWNSTONE HOUSE – NIGHT

Bud comes out the door, in slippered feet, pants and raincoat over his pajamas. As he sleep-walks down the steps, a cab pulls up in front of the house. Bud ducks discreetly into the areaway. Mr. Dobisch, bareheaded, emerges cautiously from the cab. Between the fingers of his hands he is carrying four long-stemmed glasses, brimful of stingers. The blonde steps out, holding his hat.
BLONDE: This the place?
DOBISCH: Yeah. (*to cab driver*): How much?
CABBIE: Seventy cents. *Dobisch, his hands full of stingers, turns to the blonde, indicates his pants pocket.*
DOBISCH: Get the money, will you? *The blonde plants the hat on top of his head, unbuttons his overcoat, reaches into his pants pocket. As she does so, she jogs his elbow.*
DOBISCH: Watch those stingers!
The blonde has taken out Dobisch's money clip, with about a hundred dollars in it.
DOBISCH: Give him a buck.
The blonde peels a bill off, hands it to the cabbie, hangs on to the rest of the roll just a second too long.
DOBISCH: Now put it back honey. (*she does*) Atta girl.

The cab drives off. Dobisch and the blonde start up the steps to the house.

BLONDE: You sure this is a good idea?

DOBISCH: Can't think of a better one.

BLONDE (*holding door open for him*): I mean – barging in on your mother – in the middle of the night?

DOBISCH (*edging past her with stingers*): Don't worry about the old lady. One squawk from her, and she's out of a job.

In the areaway, Bud has overheard them, and it doesn't make him any happier. He steps out on the sidewalk, shuffles down the street.

32   INT. SECOND FLOOR LANDING – NIGHT

The blonde and Dobisch, his hands full of stingers, come up to Bud's door.

DOBISCH: Get the key, will you.

Automatically she reaches into his pocket.

DOBISCH: Not there. Under the mat.

BLONDE (*puzzled*): Under the mat? (*picks up key*)

DOBISCH (*impatiently*): Open up, open up – we haven't got all night.

The blonde unlocks the door to the apartment, opens it.

BLONDE (*suspiciously*): So this is your mother's apartment?

DOBISCH: That's right. Maria Ouspenskaya.

BLONDE (*sticking her head in*): Hiya, Ouspenskaya.

Dobisch nudges her inside with his knee, follows, kicks the door shut behind him.

The landing is empty for a second. Then the door of the rear apartment opens, and Dr. Dreyfuss, in a beaten bathrobe, sets out a couple of empty milk bottles with a note in them. Suddenly, from Bud's apartment, comes a shrill female giggle. Dr. Dreyfuss reacts. Then the cha cha music starts full blast.

DR. DREYFUSS (*calling to his wife, off-scene*): Mildred – he's at it again.

Shaking his head, he closes the door.

33   EXT. CENTRAL PARK – NIGHT

Bud in raincoat and slippered feet, turns in off the street, plods along a path in the deserted park. He stops at a damp bench under a lamp post, sits. In the background, lights shine from the towering buildings on Central Park South.

Bud huddles inside his raincoat, shivering. He is very sleepy by now. His eyes close and his head droops. A gust of wind sends wet leaves swirling across the bench. Bud doesn't stir. He is all in.

FADE OUT.

FADE IN:

34   INT. LOBBY INSURANCE
BUILDING – DAY

It's a quarter to nine of a gray November morning, and work-bound employees are piling in through the doors. Among them is Bud, bundled up in a raincoat, hat, heavy muffler and wool gloves, and carrying a box of Kleenex. He coughs, pulls out a tissue, wipes his dripping nose. He has a bad cold.

The lobby is an imposing marbled affair, as befits a company which last year wrote 9.3 billion dollars worth of insurance. There are sixteen

elevators, *eight of them marked LOCAL-FLOORS 1-18, and opposite them eight marked EXPRESS – FLOORS 18-37. The starter, a uniformed Valkyrie wielding a clicker, is directing the flow of traffic into the various elevators.*
Bud joins the crowd in front of the express elevators. Also standing there is Mr. Kirkeby, reading the Herald-Tribune.

BUD (*hoarsely*): Good morning, Mr. Kirkeby.

KIRKEBY (*as if he just knew him vaguely*): Oh, how are you, Baxter. They keeping you busy these days?

BUD: Yes, sir. They are indeed. (*he sniffs*)

The elevator doors open, revealing the operator. She is in her middle twenties and her name is FRAN KUBELIK. *Maybe it's the way she's put together, maybe it's her face, or maybe it's just the uniform – in any case, there is something very appealing about her. She is also an individualist – she wears a carnation in her lapel, which is strictly against regulations. As the elevator loads, she greets the passengers cheerfully.*

FRAN (*rattling it off*): Morning, Mr. Kessel – Morning, Miss Robinson – Morning, Mr. Kirkeby – Morning, Mr. Williams – Morning, Miss Livingston – Morning, Mr. McKellway – Morning, Mr. Pirelli – Morning, Mrs. Schubert – *Interspersed is an occasional 'Morning, Miss*

Kubelik' *from the passengers.*

FRAN: Morning, Mr. Baxter.

BUD: Morning, Miss Kubelik.

He takes his hat off – he is the only one. The express is now loaded.

STARTER (*working the clicker*): That's all. Take it away.

FRAN (*shutting the door*): Watch the door, please Blasting off.

35   INT. ELEVATOR

Bud is standing right next to Fran as the packed express shoots up.

BUD (*studying her*): What did you do to your hair?

FRAN: It was making me nervous, so I chopped it off. Big mistake, huh?

BUD: I sort of like it.

He sniffs, takes out a Kleenex, wipes his nose.

FRAN: Say, you got a lulu.

BUD: Yeah. I better not get too close.

FRAN: Oh, I never catch colds.

BUD: Really? I was looking at some figures from the Sickness and Accident Claims Division – do you know that the average New Yorker between the ages of twenty and fifty has two and a half colds a year?

FRAN: That makes me feel just terrible.

BUD: Why?

FRAN: Well, to make the figures come out even – since I have *no* colds a year – some poor slob must have *five* colds a year.

BUD: That's me. (*dabs his nose*)

FRAN: You should have stayed in bed this morning.

BUD: I should have stayed in bed last night.

The elevator has slowed down, now stops. Fran opens the door.

FRAN: Nineteen. Watch your step.

About a third of the passengers get out, including Bud and Mr. Kirkeby. As Kirkeby passes Fran, he slaps her behind with his folded newspaper. Fran jumps slightly.

FRAN (*all in the day's work*): And watch your hand, Mr. Kirkeby!

KIRKEBY (*innocently*): I beg your pardon?

FRAN: One of these days I'm going to shut those doors on you and –

She withdraws her hand into the sleeve of her uniform, and waves the 'amputated' arm at him.

FRAN: Twenty next.

The doors close.

36 INT. NINETEENTH FLOOR – DAY

Kirkeby turns away from the elevator, and grinning smugly, falls in beside Bud.

KIRKEBY: That Kubelik – boy! Would I like to get her on a slow elevator to China.

BUD: Oh, yes. She's the best operator in the building.

KIRKEBY: I'm a pretty good operator myself – but she just won't give me a tumble – date-wise.

BUD: Maybe you're using the wrong approach.

KIRKEBY: A lot of guys around here have tried it – all kinds of approaches – no dice. What is she trying to prove?

BUD: Could be she's just a nice, respectable girl – there are millions of them.

KIRKEBY: Listen to him. Little Lord Fauntleroy!

Leaving Bud at the employees' coat-racks, Kirkeby heads toward his office, one of the glass-enclosed cubicles. Bud hangs up his hat and raincoat, stows away the gloves and muffler. Out of his coat pocket he takes a plastic anti-histamine sprayer and a box of cough drops, and still carrying the Kleenex, threads his way to his desk. Most of the desks are already occupied, and the others are filling rapidly.

Once seated at his desk, Bud arranges his medicaments neatly in front of him. He takes a Kleenex out of the box, blows his nose, then leaning back in his swivel chair sprays first one nostril, then the other. Suddenly the piercing bell goes off – the workday has begun. Being the ultra-conscientious type, Bud instantly sits upright in his chair, removes the cover from his computing machine, picks up a batch of perforated premium cards, starts entering figures on his computer.

After a few seconds, he glances around to make sure that everybody in the vicinity is busy. Then he looks up a number in the company telephone directory, dials furtively.

BUD (*cupping hand over phone mouthpiece*): Hello, Mr. Dobisch? This is Baxter, on the nineteenth floor.

37 INT. DOBISCH'S OFFICE – DAY

It is a glass-enclosed cubicle on the twenty-first

floor. Through the glass we see another enormous layout of desks, everybody working away. Dobisch is holding the phone in one hand, running an electric shaver over his face in the other.

DOBISCH: Oh, Buddy-boy. I was just about to call you. *(shuts off electric shaver)* I'm sorry about that mess on the living room wall. You see, my little friend, she kept insisting Picasso was a bum – so she started to do that mural – but I'm sure it will wash off – just eyebrow pencil.

38 BUD – ON PHONE
BUD: It's not Picasso I'm calling about. It's the key – to my apartment – you were supposed to leave it under the mat.

39 DOBISCH – ON PHONE
DOBISCH: I did, didn't I? I distinctly remember bending over and putting it there –

40 BUD ON PHONE
BUD: Oh, I found a key there, all right – only it's the wrong key.

41 DOBISCH – ON PHONE
DOBISCH: It is? *(takes Bud's key out of his pocket)* Well, how about that? No wonder I couldn't get into the executive washroom this morning.

42 BUD – ON PHONE
BUD: And I couldn't get into my apartment – so at four a.m. I had to wake up the landlady and give her a whole song and dance about going out to mail a letter and the door slamming shut.

43 DOBISCH – ON PHONE
DOBISCH: That's a shame. I'll send the key right down. And about your promotion – *(leafs through report on desk)* – I'm sending that efficiency report right up to Mr. Sheldrake, in Personnel. I wouldn't be surprised if you heard from him before the day is over.

44 BUD – ON PHONE
BUD: Thank you, Mr. Dobisch.
He hangs up, feels his forehead. It is warm. Clipped to his handkerchief pocket are a black fountain pen and, next to it, a thermometer in a black case. Bud unclips the thermometer case, unscrews the cap, shakes the thermometer out, puts it under his tongue. He resumes work.
A messenger comes up to his desk with an inter-office envelope.
MESSENGER: From Mr. Dobisch.
BUD *(thermometer in mouth)*: Wait.
He turns away from the messenger, unties the string of the envelope, takes his key out, puts it in a coat pocket. From a trouser pocket, he extracts Dobisch's key to the executive washroom, slips it discreetly into the envelope, reties it, hands it to the messenger.
BUD *(thermometer in mouth)*: To Mr. Dobisch.
Puzzled by the whole procedure, the messenger leaves. Bud now removes the thermometer from

his mouth, reads it. *It's worse than he thought. He puts the thermometer back in the case, clips it to his pocket, takes his desk calendar out of a drawer, turns a leaf. Under the date* WEDNES-DAY, NOVEMBER 4 *there is an entry in his handwriting* – MR. VANDERHOF. *Bud consults the telephone directory again, picks up the phone, dials.*

45 INT. VANDERHOF'S OFFICE – DAY

This is another glass-enclosed cubicle on another floor. MR. VANDERHOF, *a Junior Chamber of Commerce type, is dictating to an elderly secretary who sits across the desk from him.*

VANDERHOF: Dear Mr. MacIntosh – (*phone rings and he picks it up*) Vanderhof, Public Relations. Oh, yes, Baxter. Just a minute. (*to secretary*) All right, Miss Finch – type up what we got so far. (*he waits till she is out of the office; then, into phone*) Now what is it, Baxter?

46   BUD – ON PHONE

BUD: Look, Mr. Vanderhof – I've got you down here for tonight – but I'm going to be using the place myself – so I'll have to cancel.

47   VANDERHOF – ON PHONE

VANDERHOF: Cancel? But it's her birthday – I already ordered the cake –

48   BUD – ON PHONE

BUD: I hate to disappoint you – I mean, many happy returns – but not tonight –

49   VANDERHOF – ON PHONE

VANDERHOF: That's not like you, Baxter. Just the other day, at the staff meeting, I was telling Mr. Sheldrake what a reliable man you were.

50   BUD – ON PHONE

BUD: Thank you, Mr. Vanderhof. But I'm sick – I have this terrible cold – and a fever – and I got to go to bed right after work.

51   VANDERHOF – ON PHONE

VANDERHOF: Buddy-boy, that's the worst thing you can do. If you got a cold, you should go to a Turkish bath – spend the night there – sweat it out –

52   BUD – ON PHONE

BUD: Oh, no. I'd get pneumonia – and if I got pneumonia, I'd be in bed for a month – and if I were in bed for a month –

53   VANDERHOF – ON PHONE

VANDERHOF: Okay, you made your point. We'll ust have to do it *next* Wednesday – that's the only night of the week I can get away.

54   BUD – ON PHONE

BUD: Wednesday – Wednesday – (*leafing through calendar*) I got somebody pencilled in –

let me see what I can do – I'll get back to you. *He hangs up, riffles through the directory, finds the number, and with a furtive look around, dials again.*

BUD (*into phone*): Mr. Eichelberger? Is this Mortgage and Loan? I'd like to speak to Mr. Eichelberger. Yes, it *is* urgent.

55   INT. EICHELBERGER'S OFFICE – DAY

Also glass-enclosed, but slightly larger than the others. MR EICHELBERGER, a solid citizen of about fifty, is displaying some mortgage graphs to three associates. A fourth one has answered the phone.

ASSOCIATE (*holding out phone to Eichelberger*): For you, Mel.
Eichelberger puts the charts down, takes the phone.

EICHELBERGER: Eichelberger here – oh, yes, Baxter – (*a glance at his associates; then continues, as though it were a business call*) What's

your problem? – Wednesday is out? – oh – that throws a little monkey wrench into my agenda – Thursday? No, I'm all tied up on Thursday – let's schedule that meeting for Friday.

56 BUD – ON PHONE

BUD: Friday? (*checks calendar*) Let me see what I can do. I'll get back to you.
He hangs up, consults the directory, starts to dial a number.

57 INT. KIRKEBY'S OFFICE – DAY

It's another of those glass-enclosed cubicles, on the nineteenth floor. Kirkeby is talking into a dictaphone.
KIRKEBY: Premium-wise and billing-wise, we are eighteen per cent ahead of last year, October-wise.
The phone has been ringing. Kirkeby switches off the machine, picks up the phone.
KIRKEBY: Hello? Yeah, Baxter. What's up?

58 BUD – ON PHONE

BUD: Instead of Friday – could you possibly switch to Thursday? You'd be doing me a great favor –

59 KIRKEBY – ON PHONE

KIRKEBY: Well – it's all right with *me*, Bud. Let me check. I'll get back to you.
He presses down the button on the cradle, dials Operator.

60 INT. SWITCHBOARD ROOM

There is a double switchboard in the center, with nine girls on each side, all busy as beavers. In the foreground we recognize Sylvia, Kirkeby's date of last night.
SYLVIA: Consolidated Life – I'll connect you – Consolidated Life –
The girl next to her turns and holds out a line.
SWITCHBOARD GIRL: Sylvia – it's for you.
Sylvia plugs the call into her own switchboard.

SYLVIA: Yes? Oh, hello – sure I got home all right – you owe me forty-five cents.

61 KIRKEBY – ON PHONE

KIRKEBY: Okay, okay. Look, Sylvia – instead of Friday – could we make it Thursday night?

62 SYLVIA – AT SWITCHBOARD

SYLVIA: Thursday? That's The Untouchables. – with Bob Stack.

63 KIRKEBY – ON PHONE

KIRKEBY: Bob WHO? all right, so we'll watch it at the apartment. Big deal. (*he hangs up, dials*) Baxter? It's okay for Thursday.

64 INT. NINETEENTH FLOOR – DAY

Bud, at his desk, is on the phone.
BUD: Thank you, Mr. Kirkeby. (*hangs up, consults directory, dials*) Mr. Eichelberger? It's okay for Friday. (*hangs up, consults directory, dials*) Mr. Vanderhof? It's okay for Wednesday.
During this, the phone has rung at the next desk, and the occupant, MR. MOFFETT, has picked it up. As Bud hangs up –
MOFFETT (*into phone*): All right – I'll tell him. (*hangs up, turns to Bud*) Hey, Baxter – that was Personnel. Mr. Sheldrake's secretary.
BUD: Sheldrake?
MOFFETT: She's been trying to reach you for the last twenty minutes. They want you upstairs.
BUD: Oh!
He jumps up, stuffs the nose-spray into one pocket, a handful of Kleenex into the other.
MOFFETT: What gives, Baxter? You getting promoted or getting fired?
BUD (*cockily*): Care to make a small wager?
MOFFETT: I've been here twice as long as you have –
BUD: Shall we say – a dollar?
MOFFETT: It's a bet.
Bud snake-hips between the desks like a broken-

field runner.

At the elevator, Bud presses the UP button, paces nervously. One of the elevator doors opens, and as Bud starts inside, the doors of the adjoining elevator open, and Fran Kubelik sticks her head out.

FRAN: Going up?

Hearing her voice, Bud throws a quick 'Excuse me' to the other operator, exits quickly and steps into Fran's elevator.

BUD: Twenty-seven, please. And drive carefully. You're carrying precious cargo – I mean, manpower-wise.

Fran shuts the doors.

65 INT. ELEVATOR – DAY

Fran presses a button, and the elevator starts up.

FRAN: Twenty-seven.

BUD: You may not realize it, Miss Kubelik, but I'm in the top ten – efficiency-wise – and this

may be the day – promotion-wise.

FRAN: You're beginning to sound like Mr. Kirkeby already.

BUD: Why not? Now that they're kicking me upstairs –

FRAN: Couldn't happen to a nicer guy. (*Bud beams*) You know, you're the only one around here who ever takes his hat off in the elevator.

BUD: Really?

FRAN: The characters you meet. Something happens to men in elevators. Must be the change of altitude – the blood rushes to their head, or something – boy, I could tell you stories –

BUD: I'd love to hear them. Maybe we could have lunch in the cafeteria sometime – or some evening, after work –

The elevator has stopped, and Fran opens the doors.

FRAN: Twenty-seven.

66 INT. TWENTY-SEVENTH FLOOR FOYER – DAY

It is pretty plush up here – soft carpeting and tall mahogany doors leading to the executive offices. The elevator door is open, and Bud steps out.

FRAN: I hope everything goes all right.

BUD: I hope so. (*turning back*) Wouldn't you know they'd call me on a day like this – with my cold and everything – (*fumbling with his tie*) How do I look?

FRAN: Fine. (*stepping out of elevator*) Wait.

She takes the carnation out of her lapel, starts to put it in Bud's buttonhole.

BUD: Thank you. That's the first thing I ever noticed about you – when you were still on the local elevator – you always wore a flower –

The elevator buzzer is now sounding insistently. Fran steps back inside.

FRAN: Good luck. And wipe your nose.

She shuts the doors. Bud looks after her, then takes a Kleenex out of his pocket, and wiping his nose, crosses to a glass door marked J. D.

SHELDRAKE, DIRECTOR OF PERSONNEL. He *stashes the used Kleenex away in another pocket, enters.*

67 INT. SHELDRAKE'S ANTEROOM – DAY

It is a sedate office with a secretary and a couple of typists. The secretary's name is MISS OLSEN. She is in her thirties, flaxen-haired, handsome, wears harlequin glasses, and has an incisive manner. Bud comes up to her desk.

BUD: C. C. Baxter – Ordinary Premium Account – Mr. Sheldrake called me.

MISS OLSEN: *I* called you – that is, I *tried* to call you – for twenty minutes.

BUD: I'm sorry, I –

MISS OLSEN: Go on in.

She indicates the door leading to the inner office. Bud squares his shoulders and starts in.

68 INT. SHELDRAKE'S OFFICE – DAY

Mr. Sheldrake is a $14,000 a year man, and rates a four-window office.

It is not quite an executive suite, but it is several pegs above the glass cubicles of the middle echelon. There is lots of leather, and a large desk behind which sits MR. SHELDRAKE. He is a substantial looking, authoritative man in his middle forties, a pillar of his suburban community, a blood donor and a family man. The latter is attested to by a framed photograph showing two boys, aged 8 and 10, in military school uniforms.

As Baxter comes through the door, Sheldrake is leafing through Dobisch's efficiency report. He looks up at Bud through a pair of heavy-rimmed reading glasses.

SHELDRAKE: Baxter?

BUD: Yes, sir.

SHELDRAKE (*studying him*): I was sort of wondering what you looked like. Sit down.

BUD: Yes, Mr. Sheldrake.

He seats himself on the very edge of the leather armchair facing Sheldrake.

SHELDRAKE: Been hearing some very nice things about you – here's a report from Mr. Dobisch – loyal, cooperative, resourceful –

BUD: Mr. Dobisch said that?

SHELDRAKE: And Mr. Kirkeby tells me· that several nights a week you work late at the office – without overtime.

BUD (*modestly*): Well, you know how it is – things pile up.

SHELDRAKE: Mr. Vanderhof, in Public Relations, and Mr. Eichelberger, in Mortgage and Loan – they'd both like to have you transferred to their departments.

BUD: That's very flattering.

Sheldrake puts the report down, takes off his glasses, leans across the desk toward Bud.

SHELDRAKE: Tell me, Baxter – just what is it that makes you so popular?

BUD: I don't know.

SHELDRAKE: Think.

Bud does so. For a moment, he is a picture of intense concentration. Then –

BUD: Would you mind repeating the question?

SHELDRAKE: Look, Baxter, I'm not stupid. I know everything that goes on in this building – in every department – on every floor – every day of the year.

BUD (*in a very small voice*): You do?

SHELDRAKE (*rises, starts pacing*): In 1957, we had an employee here, name of Fowler. *He* was very popular, too. Turned out he was running a bookie joint right in the Actuarial Department – tying up the switchboard, figuring the odds on our I.B.M. machines – so the day before the Kentucky Derby, I called in the Vice Squad and we raided the thirteenth floor.

BUD (*worried*): The Vice Squad?

SHELDRAKE: That's right, Baxter.

BUD: What – what's that got to do with me? I'm not running any bookie joint.

SHELDRAKE: What kind of joint *are* you running?

BUD: Sir?

SHELDRAKE: There's a certain key floating around the office – from Kirkeby to Vanderhof to Eichelberger to Dobisch – it's the key to a certain apartment – and you know who that apartment belongs to?

BUD: Who?

SHELDRAKE: Loyal, cooperative, resourceful C. C. Baxter.

BUD: Oh.

SHELDRAKE: Are you going to deny it?

BUD: No, sir. I'm not going to deny it. But if you'd just let me explain –

SHELDRAKE: You better.

BUD (*a deep breath*): Well, about six months ago – I was going to night school, taking this course in Advanced Accounting – and one of the guys in our department – he lives in Jersey – he was going to a banquet at the Biltmore – his wife was meeting him in town, and he needed someplace to change into a tuxedo – so I gave him the key – and word must have gotten around – because the next thing I knew, all sorts of guys were suddenly going to banquets – and when you give the key to one guy, you can't say no to another – and the whole thing got out of hand – pardon me.

He whips out the nasal-spray, administers a couple of quick squirts up each nostril.

SHELDRAKE: Baxter, an insurance company is founded on public trust. Any employee who conducts himself in a manner unbecoming – (*shifting into a new gear*) How many charter members are there in this little club of yours?

BUD: Just those four – out of a total of 31,259 – so actually, we can be very proud of our personnel – percentage-wise.

SHELDRAKE: That's not the point. Four rotten apples in a barrel – no matter how large the barrel – you realize that if this ever leaked out –

BUD: Oh, it won't. Believe me. And it's not going to happen again. From now on, nobody is going to use my apartment –

In his vehemence he squeezes the spray bottle, which squirts all over the desk.

SHELDRAKE: Where *is* your apartment?

BUD: West 67th Street. You have no idea what I've been going through – with the neighbors and the landlady and the liquor and the key –

SHELDRAKE: How do you work it with the key?

BUD: Well, usually I slip it to them in the office and they leave it under the mat – but never again – I can promise you that –

The phone buzzer sounds, and Sheldrake picks up the phone.

SHELDRAKE: Yes, Miss Olsen.

36

69 INT. SHELDRAKE'S ANTEROOM – DAY

Miss Olsen is on the phone.

MISS OLSEN: Mrs. Sheldrake returning your call – on two –

She presses a button down, starts to hang the phone up, glances around to see if the typists are watching, then raises the receiver to her ear and eavesdrops on the conversation.

70 INT. SHELDRAKE'S OFFICE – DAY

Sheldrake is talking into the phone.

SHELDRAKE: Yes, dear – I called you earlier – where were you? Oh, you took Tommy to the dentist –

During this, Bud has risen from his chair, started inching toward the door.

SHELDRAKE (*turning to him*): Where are you going, Baxter?

BUD: Well, I don't want to intrude – and I thought – since it's all straigthened out anyway –

SHELDRAKE: I'm not through with you yet.

BUD: Yes, sir.

SHELDRAKE (*into phone*): The reason I called is – I won't be home for dinner tonight. The branch manager from Kansas City is in town – I'm taking him to the theatre – Music Man, what else? No, don't wait up for me – 'bye, darling. (*hangs up, turns to Bud*) Tell me something, Baxter – have you seen Music Man?

BUD: Not yet. But I hear it's one swell show.

SHELDRAKE: How would you like to go tonight?

BUD: You mean – you and me? I thought you were taking the branch manager from Kansas City –

SHELDRAKE: I made other plans. You can have both tickets.

BUD: Well, that's very kind of you – only I'm not feeling well – you see, I have this cold – and I thought I'd go straight home.

SHELDRAKE: Baxter, you're not reading me. I told you I have plans.

BUD: So do I – I'm going to take four aspirins and get into bed – so you better give the tickets to somebody else –

SHELDRAKE: I'm not just *giving* those tickets, Baxter – I want to *swap* them.

BUD: Swap them? For what?

Sheldrake picks up the Dobisch reports, puts on his glasses, turns a page.

SHELDRAKE: It also says here – that you are alert, astute, and quite imaginative –

BUD: Oh? (*the dawn is breaking*) Oh!

He reaches into his coat pocket, fishes out a handful of Kleenex, and then finally the key to his apartment. He holds it up.

BUD: This?

SHELDRAKE: That's good thinking, Baxter. Next month there's going to be a shift in personnel around here – and as far as I'm concerned, you're executive material.

BUD: I am?

SHELDRAKE: Now put down the key – (*pushing a pad toward him*) – and put down the address.

Bud lays the key on the desk, unclips what he thinks is his fountain pen, uncaps it, starts writing on the pad.

BUD: It's on the second floor – my name is not on the door – it just says 2A –

Suddenly he realizes that he has been trying to write the address with the thermometer.

BUD: Oh – terribly sorry. It's that cold –

SHELDRAKE: Relax, Baxter.

BUD: Thank you, sir.

He has replaced the thermometer with the fountain pen, and is scribbling the address.

BUD: You'll be careful with the record player, won't you? And about the liquor – I ordered some this morning – but I'm not sure when they'll deliver it –

He has finished writing the address, shoves the pad over to Sheldrake.

SHELDRAKE: Now remember, Baxter – this is going to be our little secret.

BUD: Yes, of course.

SHELDRAKE: You know how people talk.

BUD: Oh, you don't have to worry –

SHELDRAKE: Not that I have anything to hide.

BUD: Oh, no sir. Certainly not. Anyway, it's none of my business – four apples, five apples – what's the difference – percentage-wise?

SHELDRAKE: (*holding out the tickets*) Here you are, Baxter. Have a nice time.

BUD: You too, sir.

Clutching the tickets, he backs out of the office.

DISSOLVE TO:

71 INT. LOBBY INSURANCE BUILDING – EVENING

It is about 6:30, and the building has pretty well emptied out by now. Bud, in raincoat and hat, is leaning against one of the marble pillars beyond the elevators. His raincoat is unbuttoned, and Fran's carnation is still in his lapel. He is looking off expectantly toward a door marked EM-PLOYEES' LOUNGE – WOMEN.

Some of the female employees are emerging, dressed for the street. Among them are Sylvia and her colleague from the switchboard.

SYLVIA: So I figure, a man in his position, he's going to take me to 21 and El Morocco – instead, he takes me to Hamburg Heaven and some schnook's apartment –

They pass Bud without paying any attention to him. Bud has heard the crack, and looks after Sylvia, a little hurt. Then he glances back toward the door of the lounge, as it opens and Fran Kubelik comes out. She is wearing a wool coat over a street dress, no hat.

FRAN (*passing Bud*): Good night.

BUD (*casually*): Good night.

She is about three paces beyond him when he suddenly realizes who it is.

BUD: Oh – Miss Kubelik. (*he rushes after her, taking off his hat*) I've been waiting for you.

FRAN: You have?

BUD: I almost didn't recognize you – this is the first time I've ever seen you in civilian clothes.
FRAN: How'd you make out on the twenty-seventh floor?
BUD: Great. Look – have you seen The Music Man?
FRAN: No.
BUD: Would you like to?
FRAN: Sure.
BUD: I thought maybe we could have a bite to eat first – and then –
FRAN: You mean tonight?
BUD: Yeah.
FRAN: I'm sorry, but I can't tonight. I'm meeting somebody.
BUD: Oh. (*a beat*) You mean – like a girl-friend?
FRAN: No. Like a man.
She proceeds across the lobby toward the street entrance, Bud following her.
BUD: I wasn't trying to be personal – it's just that the fellows in the office were wondering about you – whether you ever –
FRAN: Just tell 'em – now and then.
BUD: This date – is it just a date – or is it something serious?
FRAN: It *used* to be serious – at least *I* was – but he wasn't – so the whole thing is more or less kaputt.
BUD: Well, in that case, couldn't you –?
FRAN: I'm afraid not. I promised to have a drink with him – he's been calling me all week –
BUD: Oh, I understand.
He follows her out through the revolving doors.

72 EXT. INSURANCE BUILDING – EVENING
Fran and Bud come out.
BUD (*putting his hat on*): Well, it was just an idea – I hate to see a ticket go to waste –
FRAN (*stops*): What time does the show go on?
BUD: Eight-thirty.
FRAN: (*looks at her watch*) Well – I could meet you at the theatre – if that's all right.
BUD: All right? That's wonderful! It's the Majestic – 44th Street.
FRAN: Meet you in the lobby. Okay?
Bud nods happily, falls in beside her as she starts down the street.
BUD: You know, I felt lousy this morning – a hundred and one fever – then my promotion came up – now you and I – eleventh row center – and you said I should have stayed in bed.
FRAN: How *is* your cold?
BUD (*high as a kite*): What cold? And after the show, we could go out on the town – (*does a little cha cha step*) I've been taking from Arthur Murray.
FRAN: So I see.
BUD: They got a great little band at El Chico, in the Village – it's practically around the corner from where you live.
FRAN: Sounds good. (*a sudden thought*) How do you know where I live?
BUD: Oh, I even know who you live *with* – your sister and brother-in-law – I know when you were born – and where – I know all sorts of things about you.
FRAN: How come?
BUD: A couple of months ago I looked up your card in the group insurance file.
FRAN: Oh.
BUD: I know your height, your weight and your Social Security number – you had mumps, you had measles and you had your appendix out.
They have now reached the corner, and Fran stops.
FRAN: Well, don't tell the fellows in the office about the appendix. They may get the wrong idea how you found out. (*turning the corner*) 'Bye.
BUD (*calling after her*): Eight-thirty!
He watches her walk away, an idiot grin on his face. Despite what he told Fran, his nose is

stuffed up, so he takes out the anti-histamine and sprays his nostrils. Then, carried away, he squirts some of the stuff on the carnation in his buttonhole, moves off in the opposite direction.

73 EXT. DOWNTOWN STREET – EVENING

Fran comes hurrying along the street. She is late. Her objective is a small Chinese restaurant, with a neon sign reading THE RICKSHAW – COCKTAILS – CANTONESE FOOD. *She starts down a flight of steps leading to the entrance.*

74 INT. CHINESE RESTAURANT – EVENING

The bar is a long, narrow, dimly-lit room with booths along one side. Beyond a bamboo curtain is the main dining room, which does not concern us. The place is decorated in Early Beachcomber style – rattan, fish-nets, conch-shells, etc.

The help is Chinese. At this early hour, there are only half a dozen customers in the place – all at the bar except for one man, sitting in the last booth with his back toward camera. At a piano, a Chinese member of Local 808 is improvizing mood music.

Fran comes through the door, and without looking around, heads straight for the last booth. The bartender nods to her – they know her there. As she passes the piano player, he gives her a big smile, segues into JEALOUS LOVER.

Fran comes up to the man sitting in the last booth.

FRAN (*a wistful smile*): Good evening, Mr. Sheldrake.

Sheldrake, for that's who it is, looks around nervously to make sure no one has heard her.

SHELDRAKE: Please, Fran – not so loud. (*he gets up*)

FRAN: Still afraid somebody may see us together?

SHELDRAKE (*reaching for her coat*): Let me take that.

FRAN: No, Jeff. I can't stay very long. (*sits opposite him, with her coat on*) Can I .have a frozen daiquiri?

SHELDRAKE: It's on the way. (*sits down*) I see you went ahead and cut your hair.

FRAN: That's right.

SHELDRAKE: You know I liked it better long.

FRAN: Yes, I know. You want a lock to carry in your wallet?

A waiter comes up with a tray: two daiquiris, fried shrimp, eggrolls, and a bowl of sauce.

WAITER (*showing all his teeth*): Evening, lady. Nice see you again.

FRAN: Thank you.

The waiter has set everything on the table, leaves.

SHELDRAKE: How long has it been – a month?

FRAN: Six weeks. But who's counting?

SHELDRAKE: I missed you, Fran.

FRAN: Like old times. Same booth, same song –

SHELDRAKE: It's been hell.

FRAN (*dipping shrimp*): – same sauce – sweet and sour.

SHELDRAKE: You don't know what it's like – standing next to you in that elevator, day after day – Good morning, Miss Kubelik – Good night, Mr. Sheldrake – I'm still crazy about you, Fran.

FRAN (*avoiding his eyes*): Let's not start on that again, Jeff – *please*. I'm just beginning to get over it.

SHELDRAKE: I don't believe you.

FRAN: Look, Jeff – we had two months this summer – and that was it. Happens all the time – the wife and kids go away to the country, and the boss has a fling with the secretary – or the manicurist – or the elevator girl. Comes September, the picnic is over – goodbye. The kids go back to school, the boss goes back to the wife, and the girl – (*she is barely able to control herself*) They don't make these shrimp like they used to.

SHELDRAKE: I never said goodbye, Fran.

FRAN (*not listening*): For a while there, you try kidding yourself that you're going with an

40

unmarried man. Then one day he keeps looking at his watch, and aks you if there's any lipstick showing, then rushes off to catch the seven-fourteen to White Plains. So you fix yourself a cup of instant coffee – and you sit there by yourself – and you think – and it all begins to look so ugly –
There are tears in her eyes. She breaks off, downs what's left of the daiquiri.
SHELDRAKE: How do you think *I* felt – riding home on that seven-fourteen train?
FRAN: Why do you keep calling me, Jeff? What do you want from me?

SHELDRAKE (*taking her hand*): I want you back, Fran.
FRAN (*withdrawing her hand*): Sorry, Mr. Sheldrake – I'm full up. You'll have to take the next elevator.
SHELDRAKE: You're not giving me a chance, Fran. I asked you to meet me because – I have something to tell you.
FRAN: Go ahead – tell me.
SHELDRAKE (*a glance around*): Not here, Fran. Can't we go some place else?
FRAN: No. I have a date at eight-thirty.
SHELDRAKE: Important?

FRAN: Not very – but I'm going to be there anyway.

She takes out an inexpensive square compact with a fleur de lis pattern on it, opens it, starts to fix her face. The waiter comes up with a couple of menus.

WAITER: You ready order dinner now?

FRAN: No. No dinner.

SHELDRAKE: Bring us two more drinks.

CUT TO:

75 EXT. MAJESTIC THEATRE – EVENING

It is 8:25, and there is the usual hectic to-do – taxis pulling up, people milling around the sidewalk and crowding into the lobby. In the middle of this mêlée, buffeted by the throng, stands Bud, in raincoat and hat, looking anxiously for Fran.

CUT TO:

76 INT. CHINESE RESTAURANT – EVENING

Fran and Sheldrake, in the booth, are working on the second round of drinks.

SHELDRAKE: Fran – remember that last weekend we had?

FRAN (*wryly*): Do I. That leaky little boat you rented – and me in a black negligee and a life preserver –

SHELDRAKE: Remember what we talked about?

FRAN: We talked about a lot of things.

SHELDRAKE: I mean – about my getting a divorce.

FRAN: *We* didn't talk about it – *you* did.

SHELDRAKE: You didn't really believe me, did you?

FRAN (*shrugging*): They got it on a long playing record now – Music to String Her Along By. My wife doesn't understand me – We haven't gotten along for years – You're the best thing that ever happened to me –

SHELDRAKE: That's enough, Fran.

FRAN (*going right on*): Just trust me, baby –

we'll work it out somehow –

SHELDRAKE: You're not being funny.

FRAN: I wasn't trying.

SHELDRAKE: If you'll just listen to me for a minute –

FRAN: Okay. I'm sorry.

SHELDRAKE: I saw my lawyer this morning – I wanted his advice – about the best way to handle it –

FRAN: Handle what?

SHELDRAKE: What do you think?

FRAN (*looking at him for a long moment – then*): Let's get something straight, Jeff – I never asked you to leave your wife.

SHELDRAKE: Of course not. You had nothing to do with it.

FRAN (*her eyes misting up again*): Are you sure that's what you want?

SHELDRAKE: I'm sure. If you'll just tell me that you still love me –

FRAN (*softly*): You know I do.

SHELDRAKE: Fran –

He takes her hand, kisses it. The bar has been filling up, and now two couples are seating themselves in a nearby booth. One of the women is Miss Olsen.

FRAN (*pulling her hand away gently*): Jeff – darling –

She indicates the other customers. Sheldrake glances over his shoulder.

SHELDRAKE: It *is* crowding up. Let's get out of here.

They rise. Sheldrake leaves some money on the table, leads Fran toward the entrance. As they pass Miss Olsen's booth, she turns around slowly, and putting on her glasses, looks after them.

Sheldrake slips a bill to the piano player, who gives them a big smile, slides into JEALOUS LOVER again. Retrieving his hat and coat from the checkroom girl, Sheldrake steers Fran through the door.

Miss Olsen watches them with a cold smile.

77 EXT. CHINESE RESTAURANT –
EVENING

Fran and Sheldrake come up the steps.
SHELDRAKE (*to a passing cab*): Taxi!
It passes without stopping.
FRAN: I have that date – remember?
SHELDRAKE: I love you – remember?
*Another taxi approaches. Sheldrake gives a shrill
whistle, and it pulls up. He opens the door.*
FRAN: Where are we going, Jeff? Not back to
that leaky boat –
SHELDRAKE: I promise.
*He helps her into the cab, takes out of his coat
pocket the page from the pad on which Bud wrote
the address of the apartment.*
SHELDRAKE (*to cab driver*): 51 West Sixty-
Seventh.
*He gets in beside Fran, shuts the door. As the cab
pulls away, through the rear window the two can
be seen kissing.*   CUT TO:

78 EXT. MAJESTIC THEATRE –
EVENING

*It's 9 o'clock, the lobby is deserted, and standing
on the sidewalk all by himself, is Bud. He takes a
Kleenex out of his pocket, blows his nose, stuffs the
used Kleenex in another pocket. He looks up and
down the street, consults his watch, decides to wait
just a little longer.*   FADE OUT:

FADE IN:
79 BAXTER'S DESK CALENDAR
*The leaves are flipping over. Mr. Sheldrake
seems to be using The Apartment regularly – for
the name Sheldrake, in Bud's handwriting,
appears on the pages dated Monday, November 9,
Thursday, November 12, Thursday, November
19, Monday, November 23, and Monday,
November 30. Mr. Sheldrake also seems to be
Baxter's only customer by now, since the other
leaves of the calendar are blank.*

DISSOLVE TO:

80 INT. NINETEENTH FLOOR –
INSURANCE BUILDING – DAY
*It is a gloomy December morning, and hundreds of
desk-bound employees are bent over their paper-
work.*
*Bud Baxter, in raincoat and hat, is clearing out
his desk. He has piled everything on his blotter
pad – reference books, papers, a fountain pen set,
pencils, paper clips and the calendar. Watching
him from the next desk is a dumbfounded Moffett.
Bud picks up the blotter pad with his stuff on it,
and as he moves past Moffett's desk, Moffett
takes out a dollar bill, drops it grudgingly on the
loaded pad. Bud flashes him a little grin, continues between the desks toward the row of glass-
enclosed offices housing the supervisory personnel.
He comes up to an unoccupied cubicle. A sign
painter is brushing in some new lettering on the
glass door – it reads C. C. BAXTER, Second
Administrative Assistant. Bud studies the sign
with a good deal of satisfaction.*

BUD (*to painter*): *Would you mind* – ? (*the painter turns around*) C. C. Baxter – that's me. *With an 'Oh', the painter opens the door for him.*

81   INT. BAXTER'S OFFICE – DAY

Bud enters his new office, deposits his stuff on the bare desk, looks around possessively. The small cubicle boasts one window, carpeting on the floor, a filing cabinet, a couple of synthetic-leather chairs, and a clothes-tree – to Bud, it is the Taj Mahal. He crosses to the clothes-tree, removes his hat and coat, hangs them up. From OFF comes –

KIRKEBY'S VOICE: Hi, Buddy-boy.

DOBISCH'S VOICE: Congratulations, and all that jazz.

Bud turns. Kirkeby, Dobisch, Eichelberger and Vanderhof have come into the office.

BUD: Hi, fellas.

EICHELBERGER: Well, you made it, kid – just like we promised.

VANDERHOF: Quite an office – name on the door – rug on the floor – the whole schmear.

BUD: Yeah.

DOBISCH: Teamwork – that's what counts in an organization like this. All for one and one for all – know what I mean?

BUD: I have a vague idea.

Kirkeby signals to Vanderhof, who shuts the door.

The four charter members of the club start closing in on Bud.

KIRKEBY: Baxter, we're a little disappointed in you – gratitude-wise.

BUD: Oh, I'm very grateful.

EICHELBERGER: Then why are you locking us out, all of a sudden?

BUD: It's been sort of rough these last few weeks – what with my cold and like that –

He has picked up the desk calendar, shoves it discreetly into one of the drawers.

DOBISCH: We went to bat for you – and now you won't play ball with us.

BUD: Well, after all, it's my apartment – it's private property – it's not a public playground.

VANDERHOF: All right, so you got yourself a girl – that's okay with us – but not every night of the week.

KIRKEBY: How selfish can you get? (*to the others*) Last week I had to borrow my nephew's car and take Sylvia to a drive-in in Jersey. I'm too old for that sort of thing – I mean, in a Volkswagen.

BUD: I sympathize with your problem – and believe me, I'm very sorry –

DOBISCH: You'll be a lot sorrier before we're through with you.

BUD: You threatening me?

DOBISCH: Listen, Baxter, we made you and we can break you.

He deliberately flips a cigar ash on Bud's desk. At the same time, the door opens, and Sheldrake comes striding in briskly.

BUD: Good morning, Mr. Sheldrake.

The others swivel around.

SHELDRAKE: Morning, gentlemen. (*to Bud*) Everything satisfactory? You like your office?

BUD: Oh, yes, sir. Very much. And I want to thank you –

SHELDRAKE: Don't thank me – thank your friends here – they're the ones who recommended you.

The four friends manage to work up some sickly

smiles.

DOBISCH: We just dropped in to wish him the best. (*quickly brushes cigar ash off the desk*).
KIRKEBY (*as they move toward the door*): So long, Baxter. We know you won't let us down.
BUD: So long, fellas. Drop in any time. The door is always open – to my office.
They leave. Sheldrake and Bud are alone.
SHELDRAKE: I like the way you handled that. Well, how does it feel to be an executive?
BUD: Fine. And I want you to know I'll work very hard to justify your confidence in me –
SHELDRAKE: Sure you will. (*a beat*) Say, Baxter, about the apartment – now that you got a raise, don't you think we can afford a *second* key?
BUD: Well – I guess so.
SHELDRAKE: You know my secretary – Miss Olsen –
BUD: Oh, yes. Very attractive. Is she – the lucky one?
SHELDRAKE: No, you don't understand. She's a busybody – always poking her nose into things – and with that key passing back and forth – why take chances?
BUD: Yes, sir. You can't be too careful.
He glances towards the glass partitions to make sure that nobody is watching.
BUD: I have something here – I think it belongs to you.
Out of his pocket he has slipped the compact with the fleur-de-lis pattern we saw Fran use at the Rickshaw. He holds it out to Sheldrake.
SHELDRAKE: To me?
BUD: I mean – the young lady – whoever she may be – it was on the couch when I got home last night.
SHELDRAKE: Oh, yes. Thanks.
BUD: The mirror is broken. (*opens compact, revealing crack in mirror*) It was broken when I found it.
SHELDRAKE: So it was. (*takes the compact*) She threw it at me.

BUD: Sir?
SHELDRAKE: You know how it is – sooner or later they all give you a bad time.
BUD (*man-of-the-world*): I know how it is.
SHELDRAKE: You see a girl a couple of times a week – just for laughs – and right away she thinks you're going to divorce your wife. I ask you – is that fair?
BUD: No, sir. That's very unfair – especially to your wife.
SHELDRAKE: Yeah. (*shifting gears*) You know, Baxter, I envy you. Bachelor – all the dames you want – no headaches, no complications –
BUD: Yes, sir. That's the life, all right.
SHELDRAKE: Put me down for Thursday again.
BUD: Roger. And I'll get that other key.
Sheldrake exits. Bud takes the calendar out of the desk drawer, makes an entry.

DISSOLVE TO:

82   BAXTER'S DESK CALENDAR
Again the leaves are flipping over, and again we see Sheldrake's name in Bud's handwriting – booked for the following dates: Monday, December 14, Thursday, December 17, Monday, December 21, Thursday, December 24.

DISSOLVE TO:

83   INT. SWITCHBOARD ROOM – DAY
Perched on top of the switchboard is a small decorated Christmas tree, and the operators are dispensing holiday greetings to all callers.
OPERATORS: Consolidated Life – Merry Christmas – I'll connect you – Consolidated Life – Merry Christmas – I'm ringing –
In the foreground, Sylvia is engaged in a private conversation of her own.
SYLVIA (*into mouthpiece*): Yeah? – YEAH? – Where? – You bet –
She tears off the headset, and turns to the other girls.
SYLVIA: Somebody watch my line – there's a

45

swinging party up on the nineteenth floor –

She scoots out the door. The other girls immediately abandon their posts, and dash after her.

84   INT. NINETEENTH FLOOR – DAY

It's a swinging party, all right. Nobody is working. Several desks have been cleared and pushed together, and on top of this improvized stage four female employees and Mr. Dobisch, with his pants-legs rolled up, are doing a Rockette kick routine to the tune of JINGLE BELLS. *Employees are ringed around the performers, some drinking out of paper cups, others singing and clapping in rhythm.*

One of the cubicles has been transformed into a bar, and it is jammed with people. Mr. Kirkeby and Mr. Vanderhof are pouring – each has a couple of bottles of liquor in his hands, and is emptying them into the open top of a watercooler. But the stuff is flowing out as fast as it flows in – everybody is in line with a paper cup waiting for a refill.

Bud comes shouldering his way out of the crowded cubicle, holding aloft two paper cups filled with booze. Since his promotion he has bought himself a new suit, dark flannel, and with it he wears a white shirt with a pinned round collar, and a foulard tie. He also has quite a glow on. Detouring past necking couples, he heads in the direction of the elevators.

The doors of Fran's elevator are just opening, and the switchboard operators, led by Sylvia, come streaming out.

SYLVIA (*to a colleague*): – so I said to him: Never again! – either get yourself a bigger car or a smaller girl –

As they head for the party, they pass Bud, who is approaching the elevator with the two drinks. Fran is just closing the elevator doors.

BUD: Miss Kubelik.

The doors slide open again, and Fran looks out. Instead of the customary carnation in the lapel of her uniform, she wears a sprig of holly.

BUD (*holding out one of the drinks*): Merry Christmas.
FRAN: Thank you. (*takes drink*) I thought you were avoiding me.
BUD: What gave you that idea?
FRAN: In the last six weeks you've only been in my elevator once – and then you didn't take your hat off.
BUD: Well, as a matter of fact, I *was* rather hurt when you stood me up that night –
FRAN: I don't blame you. It was unforgivable.
BUD: I forgive you.
FRAN: You shouldn't.

BUD: You couldn't help yourself, I mean, when you're having a drink with *one* man, you can't just suddenly walk out on him because you have *another* date with *another* man. You did the only decent thing.
FRAN: Don't be too sure. Just because I wear a uniform – that doesn't make me a Girl Scout.
BUD: Miss Kubelik, one doesn't get to be a second administrative assistant around here unless he's a pretty good judge of character – and as far as I'm concerned, you're tops. I mean decency-wise – and otherwise-wise. (*toasting*) Cheers.
FRAN: Cheers.
They down their drinks. Bud takes the empty cup from her.
BUD: One more?
FRAN (*indicating elevator*): I shouldn't drink when I'm driving.
BUD: You're so right.
He reaches into the elevator, takes a cardboard sign off a hook, hangs it on the elevator door. It reads USE OTHER ELEVATOR.
BUD: By the power vested in me, I herewith declare this elevator out of order. (*leading her toward the party*) Shall we join the natives?
FRAN: Why not? (*as they pass a kissing couple*) They seem friendly enough.
BUD: Don't you believe it. Later on there will be human sacrifices – white collar workers tossed into the computing machines, and punched full of those little square holes.
FRAN: How many of those drinks did you have?
BUD (*holding up four fingers*): Three.
FRAN: I thought so.
They have now reached the entrance to the bar, which is overflowing with thirsty natives.
BUD: You wait here. I think I hear the sound of running water.
He leaves her outside the cubicle, and elbows his way through the crowd toward the booze-filled water cooler. Out of another cubicle comes Miss

47

Olsen, cup in hand. She too has had quite a few. Seeing Fran, she walks up to her, with an acid smile on her face.

MISS OLSEN: Hi. How's the branch manager from Kansas City?

FRAN: I beg your pardon?

MISS OLSEN: I'm Miss Olsen – Mr. Sheldrake's secretary.

FRAN: Yes, I know.

MISS OLSEN: So you don't have to play innocent

with me. He used to tell his wife that I was the branch manager from Seattle – four years ago when *we* were having a little ring-a-ding-ding.

FRAN: I don't know what you're talking about.

MISS OLSEN: And before me there was Miss Rossi in Auditing – and after me there was Miss Koch in Disability – and just before you there was Miss What's-Her-Name, on the twenty-fifth floor –

FRAN (*wanting to get away*): Will you excuse

me?

MISS OLSEN (*holding her by the arm*): What for?
You haven't done anything – it's him – what a
salesman – always the last booth in the Chinese
restaurant – and the same pitch about divorcing
his wife – and in the end you wind up with egg
foo yong on your face.

*Bud comes burrowing out of the crowded cubicle,
balancing the two filled paper cups, spots Fran.*

BUD: Miss Kubelik.

Fran turns away from Miss Olsen.

FRAN: Well – thank you.

MISS OLSEN: Always happy to do something for
our girls in uniform.

*She moves off as Bud joins Fran, who is looking
a little pale.*

BUD: You all right? What's the matter?

FRAN: Nothing. (*takes the drink*) There are
just too many people here.

BUD: Why don't we step into my office?

There's something I want your advice about, anyway. (*leads her toward his cubicle*) I have my own office now, naturally. And you may be interested to know I'm the second youngest executive in the company – the only one younger is a grandson of the chairman of the board.

85   INT. BAXTER'S OFFICE – DAY

Bud ushers Fran in, and is confronted by a strange couple necking in the corner. He gestures them out, crosses to his desk.

BUD: Miss Kubelik, I would like your honest opinion. I've had this in my desk for a week – cost me fifteen dollars – but I just couldn't get up enough nerve to wear it –

From under the desk he has produced a hatbox, and out of the hatbox a black bowler, which he now puts on his head.

BUD: It's what they call the junior executive model. What do you think?

Fran looks at him blankly, absorbed in her own thoughts.

BUD: Guess I made a boo-boo, huh?

FRAN (*paying attention again*): No – I like it.

BUD: Really? You mean you wouldn't be ashamed to be seen with somebody in a hat like this?

FRAN: Of course not.

BUD: Maybe if I wore it a little more to the side – (*adjusting hat*) – is that better?

FRAN: Much better.

BUD: Well, as long as you wouldn't be ashamed to be seen with me – how about the three of us going out this evening – you and me and the bowler – stroll down Fifth Avenue – sort of break it in –

FRAN: This is a bad day for me.

BUD: I understand, Christmas – family and all that –

FRAN: I'd better get back to my elevator. I don't want to be fired.

BUD: Oh, you don't have to worry about that.

I have quite a bit of influence in Personnel. You know Mr. Sheldrake?

FRAN (*guardedly*): Why?

BUD: He and I are like this. (*crosses his fingers*) Sent me a Christmas card. See?

He has picked up a Christmas card from his desk, shows it to Fran. It is a photograph of the Sheldrake clan grouped around an elaborate Christmas tree – Mr. and Mrs. Sheldrake, the two boys in military school uniforms, and a big French poodle. Underneath it says:

SEASON'S GREETINGS
from the SHELDRAKES
Emily, Jeff, Tommy, Jeff Jr.,
and Figaro.

FRAN (*studying the card ruefully*): Makes a cute picture.

BUD: I thought maybe I could put in a word for you with Mr. Sheldrake – get you a little promotion – how would you like to be an elevator starter?

FRAN: I'm afraid there are too many other girls around here with seniority over me.

BUD: No problem. Why don't we discuss it sometime over the holidays – I could call you and pick you up – and we'll have the big unveiling – (*touching the brim of his bowler*) – you sure this is the right way to wear it?

FRAN: I think so.

BUD: You don't think it's tilted a little *too* much –

Fran takes her compact out of her uniform pocket, open it, hands it to Bud.

FRAN: Here.

BUD (*examining himself in the mirror*): After all, this is a conservative firm – I don't want people to think I'm an entertainer –

His voice trails off. There is something familiar about the cracked mirror of the compact – and the fleur-de-lis pattern on the case confirms his suspicion. Fran notices the peculiar expression on his face.

FRAN: What is it?

BUD (*with difficulty*): The mirror – it's broken.

FRAN: I know. I like it this way – makes me look the way I feel.

The phone has started to ring. Bud doesn't hear it. He closes the compact, hands it to Fran.

FRAN: Your phone.

BUD: Oh. (*picks up phone from desk*) Yes? (*throws a quick look at Fran*) Just a minute. (*covers the mouthpiece; to Fran*) If you don't mind – this is sort of personal.

FRAN: All right. Have a nice Christmas.

She exits, closing the door. Bud takes his hand off the mouthpiece.

BUD (*every word hurts*): Yes, Mr. Sheldrake – no, I didn't forget – the tree is up and the Tom and Jerry mix is in the refrigerator – yes, sir – same to you.

He hangs up, stands there for a moment, the bowler still on his head, the noise from the party washing over him. He slowly crosses to the clothes-tree, picks up his coat – a new, black chesterfield. With the coat over his arm, he starts out of the office.

86   INT. NINETEENTH FLOOR – DAY

The party has picked up tempo. On top of the desks, Sylvia is doing a mock strip tease – without taking any clothes off. There is hollering,

drinking and clapping all around her.

*Bud moves past the floor show, paying no atten-
tion. Kirkeby spots him, detaches himself from
the cheering section around Sylvia.*

KIRKEBY: Where you going, Buddy-boy? The
party's just starting. (*catching up with him*)
Listen, kid – give me a break, will you – how
about tomorrow afternoon? I can't take her to
that drive-in again – the car doesn't even have a
heater – four o'clock – okay?

*Bud ignores him, continues walking through the
ranks of empty desks.*

DISSOLVE TO:

87   INT. CHEAP BAR – COLUMBUS
AVENUE IN THE SIXTIES –
EVENING

*It is six o'clock, and the joint is crowded with
customers having one for the road before joining
their families for Christmas Eve. There are men
with gaily wrapped packages, small trussed-up
Christmas trees, a plucked turkey in a plastic bag.
Written across the mirror behind the bar, in
glittering white letters, is* HAPPY HOLIDAYS.
*Everybody is in high spirits, laughing it up and
toasting each other.*

*Everybody except Bud Baxter. He is standing
at the bar in his chesterfield and bowler, slightly
isolated, brooding over an almost empty martini
glass. The bartender comes up, sets down a fresh
martini with an olive on a toothpick, takes his
payment from a pile of bills and coins lying in
front of Bud. Bud fishes out the olive, adds it to
half a dozen other impaled olives neatly arranged
in fan shape on the counter. He is obviously
trying to complete the circle.*

*A short, rotund man dressed as Santa Claus
hurries in from the street, and comes up to the bar
beside Bud.*

SANTA CLAUS (*to bartender*): Hey, Charlie – give
me a shot of bourbon – and step on it – my
sleigh is double parked.

He laughs uproariously at his own joke, nudges

Bud with his elbow. Bud stares at him coldly, turns back to his martini. The laughter dies in Santa Claus' throat. He gets his shot of bourbon, moves down the bar to find more convivial company.

Standing near the end of the curved bar is a girl in her middle twenties wearing a ratty fur coat. Her name is MARGIE MACDOUGALL, *she is drinking a Rum Collins through a straw, and she too is alone. From a distance, she is studying Bud with interest. On the bar in front of her is a container of straws in paper wrappers. She takes one of them out, tears off the end of the paper, blows through the straw — sending the wrapper floating toward Bud. The paper wrapper passes right in front of Bud's nose. He doesn't notice it. Margie, undaunted, lets go with another missile. This time the wrapper lands on the brim of Bud's bowler. No reaction. Another wrapper comes floating in, hits Bud's cheek. He never takes his eye off his martini.*

Margie leaves her place, and carrying her handbag and her empty glass, comes up alongside Bud. Without a word, she reaches up and removes the wrapper from Bud's bowler.

MARGIE: You buy me a drink, I'll buy you some music. (*sets the glass down*) Rum Collins. *Not waiting for an answer, she heads for the juke box. Bud looks after her noncommittally, then turns to the bartender.*

BUD: Rum Collins. (*indicating martini glass*) And another one of these little mothers.

At the juke box, Margie has dropped a coin in and made her selection. The music starts — ADESTE FIDELIS. *She rejoins Bud at the bar just as the bartender is putting down their drinks in front of them. Bud removes the new olive, adds it to the pattern on the counter in front of him. They both drink, staring straight ahead. For quite a while, there is complete silence between them.*

MARGIE (*out of nowhere*): You like Castro? (*a blank look from Bud*) I mean – how do you feel about Castro?

BUD: What is Castro?

MARGIE: You know, that big-shot down in Cuba – with the crazy beard.

BUD: What about him?

MARGIE: Because as far as I'm concerned, he's a no good fink. Two weeks ago I wrote him a letter – never even answered me.

BUD: That so.

MARGIE: All I wanted him to do was let Mickey out for Christmas.

BUD: Who is Mickey?

MARGIE: My husband. He's in Havana – in jail.

BUD: Oh. Mixed up in that revolution?

MARGIE: Mickey? He wouldn't do nothing like that. He's a jockey. They caught him doping a horse.

BUD: Well, you can't win 'em all.

They sit there silently for a moment, contemplating the injustices of the world.

MARGIE (*to herself*):
'Twas the night before Christmas
And all through the house
Not a creature was stirring –
Nothing –
No action –
Dullsville!
(*drinks; to Bud*) You married?

BUD: No.

MARGIE: Family?

BUD: No.

MARGIE: A night like this, it sort of spooks you to walk into an empty apartment.

BUD: I said I had no family – I didn't say I had an empty apartment.

They both drink.   CUT TO:

88   INT. BUD'S APARTMENT –
      EVENING
The living room is dark, except for a shaft of light from the kitchen, and the glow of the colored bulbs on a small Christmas tree in front of the phony fireplace.
Hunched up in one corner of the couch is Fran, still in her coat and gloves, crying softly. Pacing up and down is Sheldrake. His coat and hat are on a chair, as are several Christmas packages. On the coffee table are an unopened bottle of Scotch, a couple of untouched glasses, and a bowl of melting ice.

SHELDRAKE (*stops and faces Fran*): Come on, Fran – don't be like that. You just going to sit there and keep bawling? (*no answer*) You won't talk to me, you won't tell me what's wrong – (*a new approach*) Look, I know you think I'm stalling you. But when you've been married to a woman for twelve years, you don't just sit down at the breakfast table and say 'Pass the sugar – and I want a divorce.' It's not that easy. (*he resumes pacing; Fran continues crying*) Anyway, this is the wrong time. The kids are home from school – my in-laws are visiting for the holidays – I can't bring it up *now*. (*stops in front of her*) This isn't like you, Fran – you were always such a good sport – such fun to be with –

FRAN (*through tears*): Yeah – that's me. The Happy Idiot – a million laughs.

SHELDRAKE: Well, that's more like it. At least you're speaking to me.

FRAN: Funny thing happened to me at the office party today – I ran into your secretary – Miss Olsen. You know – ring-a-ding-ding? I laughed so much I like to died.

SHELDRAKE: Is that what's bothering you – Miss Olsen? That's ancient history.

FRAN: I was never very good at history. Let me see – there was Miss Olsen, and then there was Miss Rossi – no, she came before – it was Miss Koch, who came after Miss Olsen –

SHELDRAKE: Now, Fran –

FRAN: And just think – right now there's some lucky girl in the building who's going to come after me –

SHELDRAKE: Okay, okay, Fran. I deserve that. But just ask yourself – why does a man run around with a lot of girls? Because he's unhappy at home – because he's lonely, that's why – all that was before you, Fran – I've stopped running.

Fran has taken a handkerchief out of her bag and is dabbing her eyes.

FRAN: How could I be so stupid? You'd think I would have learned by now – when you're in love with a married man, you shouldn't wear mascara.

SHELDRAKE: It's Christmas Eve, Fran – let's not fight.

FRAN: Merry Christmas.

She hands him a flat, wrapped package.

SHELDRAKE: What is it?

He strips away the wrapping to reveal a long-playing record. The cover reads: RICKSHAW BOY – *Jimmy Lee Kiang with Orchestra.*

SHELDRAKE: Oh. Our friend from the Chinese

SHELDRAKE (*grabbing her arms*): Stop that, Fran.

FRAN (*quietly*): You'll miss your train, Jeff.

Sheldrake hurriedly puts on his hat and coat, gathers up his packages.

SHELDRAKE: Coming?

FRAN: You run along – I want to fix my face.

SHELDRAKE (*heading for the door*): Don't forget to kill the lights. See you Monday.

FRAN: Sure. Monday and Thursday – and Monday again – and Thursday again –

SHELDRAKE (*that stops him in the half-open door*): It won't always be like this. (*coming back*) I love you, Fran.

Holding the packages to one side, he tries to kiss her on the mouth.

FRAN (*turning her head*): Careful – lipstick.

He kisses her on the cheek, hurries out of the apartment, closing the door. Fran stands there for a while, blinking back tears, then takes the long-playing record out of its envelope, crosses to

restaurant. Thanks, Fran. We better keep it here.

FRAN: Yeah, we better.

SHELDRAKE: I have a present for *you*. I didn't quite know what to get you – anyway it's a little awkward for me, shopping – (*he has taken out a money clip, detaches a bill*) – so here's a hundred dollars – go out and buy yourself something.

He holds the money out, but she doesn't move. Sheldrake slips the bill into her open bag.

SHELDRAKE: They have some nice alligator bags at Bergdorf's –

Fran gets up slowly and starts peeling off her gloves. Sheldrake looks at her, then glances nervously at his wrist watch.

SHELDRAKE: Fran, it's a quarter to seven – and I mustn't miss the train – if we hadn't wasted all that time – I have to get home and trim the tree –

Fran has started to remove her coat.

FRAN: Okay. (*shrugs the coat back on*) I just thought as long as it was paid for –

SHELDRAKE (*an angry step toward her*): Don't ever talk like that, Fran! Don't make yourself out to be cheap.

FRAN: A hundred dollars? I wouldn't call that cheap. And you must be paying somebody something for the use of the apartment –

the phonograph. *She puts the record on, starts the machine – the music is* JEALOUS LOVER. *As it plays, Fran wanders aimlessly around the darkened room, her body wracked by sobs. Finally she regains control of herself, and picking up her handbag, starts through the bedroom toward the bathroom.*
In the bathroom, Fran switches on the light, puts her bag on the sink, turns on the faucet. Scooping up some water, she washes the smeared mascara away, then turns the faucet off, picks up a towel. As she is drying her face, she notices in the pull-away shaving mirror the magnified reflection of a vial of pills on the medicine shelf. Fran reaches out for the vial, turns it slowly around in her hand. The label reads: SECONAL – ONE AT BEDTIME AS NEEDED FOR SLEEP.
Fran studies the label for a second, then returns the vial to the shelf. She opens her handbag, takes out a lipstick. As she does so, she sees the hundred dollar bill Sheldrake left in the bag. Her eyes

wander back to the vial on the medicine shelf. Then very deliberately she picks up Bud's mouthwash glass, removes the two toothbrushes from it, turns on the faucet, starts filling the glass with water. DISSOLVE TO:

89   INT. CHEAP BAR – COLUMBUS
      AVENUE – NIGHT
The joint is deserted now except for the Santa Claus, who is leaning against the bar, quite loaded, and Bud and Margie MacDougall, who are dancing to a slow blues coming from the juke box. Bud is still in his overcoat and bowler, and Margie is wearing her fur coat. The bartender is sweeping up the place.
BARTENDER (*to Santa Claus*): Drink up, Pop. It's closing time.
SANTA CLAUS: But it's early, Charlie.
BARTENDER: Don't you know what night this is ?
SANTA CLAUS: I know, Charlie. I know. I work for the outfit.
He polishes off his drink, walks out unsteadily. The bartender approaches the dancers.
BARTENDER: Hey, knock it off, will you ? Go home.
Bud and Margie ignore him, continue dancing – or rather swaying limply cheek-to-cheek. The bartender crosses to the juke box, pulls the plug

out. The music stops, but not Bud and Margie –
they continue dancing.

BARTENDER: O-U-T – out!

He goes to the front of the bar, starts to ex-
tinguish the lights. Margie picks up her handbag
from the bar, and Bud downs the remains of his
drink.

MARGIE: Where do we go – my place or yours?

BUD (*peering at his watch*): Might as well go to
mine – everybody else does.

He leads her through the dark bar toward the
entrance. The bartender holds the door open for
them as they go out. DISSOLVE TO:

90 EXT. BROWNSTONE HOUSE – NIGHT

Bud and Margie come walking down the street.
As they reach the house, Bud starts up the steps,
but Margie continues along the sidewalk.

MARGIE: Poor Mickey – when I think of him all
by himself in that jail in Havana – (*opening her*
handbag) – want to see his picture?

BUD (*from steps*): Not particularly.

Margie, realizing her mistake, hurries back to
join him.

MARGIE: He's so cute – five-foot-two – ninety-
nine pounds . . . like a little chihuahua.

They pass through the front door into the ves-
tibule.

91 INT. STAIRCASE – BROWNSTONE HOUSE – NIGHT

Bud and Margie are mounting the stairs toward
the apartment.

MARGIE: Can I ask you a personal question?

BUD: No.

MARGIE: You got a girl-friend?

BUD: She may be a girl – but she's no friend of
mine.

MARGIE: Still stuck on her, huh.

BUD: Stuck on her! Obviously, you don't know me very well.

MARGIE: I don't know you at all.

BUD: Permit me – C. C. Baxter – junior executive, Arthur Murray graduate, lover.

MARGIE: I'm Mrs. MacDougall – Margie to you.

Bud has taken the key out of his pocket, opened the door to his apartment.

BUD: This way, Mrs. MacDougall.

He ushers her in.

92   INT. APARTMENT – NIGHT

It is exactly the way we left it. There is no sign of Fran, except for the gloves she dropped on the coffee table earlier. Bud switches on the light, shuts the door.

MARGIE (*looking around*): Say, this is Snugsville.

BUD (*helping her out of her coat*): Mrs. Mac-Dougall, I think it is only fair to warn you that you are alone with a notorious sexpot.

MARGIE (*a gleam*): No kidding.

BUD: Ask anybody around here. As a matter of fact, when it's time for me to go – and I may go just like that – (*snaps his fingers*) – I have promised my body to the Columbia Medical Center.

MARGIE (*shuddering deliciously*): Gee. Sort of gives you goose-bumps just to think about it.

BUD: Well, they haven't got me yet, baby. Dig up some ice from the kitchen and let's not waste any time – preliminary-wise.

MARGIE: I'm with you, lover.

She takes the bowl of melted ice Bud has handed her, disappears into the kitchen. As Bud starts to remove his coat, he becomes aware of a scratching noise from the phonograph. He crosses to it, sees that the needle is stuck in the last groove of a long-playing record.

Bud lifts the record off, examines it curiously,

then puts it aside and substitutes the cha cha record. As the music starts, he dances over to the coat-rack beside the door, hangs up his chesterfield and bowler. He turns back into the room, still dancing, suddenly spots Fran's gloves on the coffee table. He picks up the gloves, looks around for some convenient place to get rid of them. Moving over to the bedroom door, he opens it, tosses the gloves toward the bed inside. He shuts the door, starts to turn away, freezes in a delayed reaction to something he saw inside. He quickly opens the door again, looks.

Sprawled across the bed, on top of the bedspread, is Fran. The light from the bathroom falls across her. She is fully dressed, still in her coat, and apparently asleep.

Bud steps into the bedroom, closing the door behind him, walks over to Fran.

BUD: All right, Miss Kubelik – get up. It's past checking-out time, and the hotel management would appreciate it if you would get the hell out of here. (Fran doesn't stir) Look, Miss Kubelik, I used to like you – I used to like you a lot – but it's all over between us – so beat it – O-U-T – out! (no reaction; he puts a hand on her shoulder, shakes her) Come on – wake up!

She doesn't respond. But something falls out of her hand, rolls across the bed. Bud picks it up, looks at it – it is his sleeping-pill vial, now un-capped and empty.

BUD (a hoarse whisper): Oh, my God.

For a second he is paralyzed. Then he drops the vial, grabs Fran, lifts her into a sitting position on the bed, shakes her violently.

BUD: Miss Kubelik! Miss Kubelik!

Fran's head droops to one side, like a rag doll's. Bud lets go of her, rushes out.

In the living room, the phonograph is still cha cha-ing away. Bud dashes to the phone, picks it up. Then it occurs to him that he doesn't know whom to call and he hangs up. Out of the kitchen comes Margie, with a bowlful of ice cubes.

MARGIE: I broke a nail trying to get the ice-tray out. You ought to buy yourself a new refriger-ator.

Bud, not listening, runs past her to the hall door and out.

MARGIE (calling after him): I didn't mean right now.

93   INT. SECOND FLOOR LANDING – NIGHT

Bud arrives at the door of the Dreyfuss apart-ment, starts ringing the doorbell and pounding with his fist.

BUD: Dr. Dreyfuss! Hey, Doc!

The door opens, and Dr. Dreyfuss stands there sleepily, pulling on his beaten bathrobe.

BUD (*words tumbling over each other*): There's a girl in my place – she took some sleeping pills – you better come quick – I can't wake her up.

DR. DREYFUSS: Let me get my bag.

He disappears from the doorway.

BUD: Hurry up, Doc.

Bud turns and runs back into his apartment.

94 INT. APARTMENT – NIGHT

Margie has settled herself comfortably on the couch, and is fixing the drinks. The cha cha music is still going. Bud comes flying in, heads for the bedroom.

MARGIE: Hey – over here, lover.

Bud stops in his tracks, suddenly aware of her.

MARGIE: What's all this running around? You're going to wear yourself out.

Bud strides over to her purposefully, yanks her up to her feet.

MARGIE: Not so rough, honey.

BUD (*taking the glass out of her hand*) Good night.

MARGIE: Good night?

BUD (*thrusting the fur coat at her*): The party's over.

MARGIE: What's the matter? Did I do something wrong?

BUD (*easing her toward door*): It's an emergency – see you some other time.

Dr. Dreyfuss comes hurrying in, carrying his medical bag. He stops, bewildered by the sound of music and the sight of a wide-awake girl in the apartment.

BUD: Not this one – (*pointing to the bedroom*) – in there, Doc.

Dr. Dreyfuss proceeds into the bedroom.

MARGIE: Say, what's going on here, anyway?

BUD: Nothing. (*propelling her toward the door*) Just clear out, will you?

MARGIE (*pointing back*): My shoes.

Bud reaches under the coffee table, where she left

her shoes, retrieves them.

MARGIE (*bitterly*): Some lover *you* are. Some sexpot!

Bud shoves the shoes at her, takes a bill out of his wallet, hands it to her.

BUD: Here – find yourself a phone booth and call your husband in Havana.

MARGIE: You bet I will. And when I tell him how you treated me, he'll push your face in. (*he shoves her through the open door*) You fink!

Bud slams the door shut, starts toward the bedroom. Halfway there, he becomes aware that the cha cha record is still on. He detours to the

phonograph, switches it off, continues into the bedroom.

In the bedroom, the overhead light is on, and Dr. Dreyfuss is working on the unconscious Fran. He has removed her coat, and is shining a flashlight into her eyes, examining her pupils. Bud approaches the bed worriedly.

BUD: She going to be all right, Doc?

DR. DREYFUSS: How many pills were in that bottle?

BUD: It was half-full – about a dozen or so. You going to have to take her to the hospital?

Dr. Dreyfuss ignores him. Out of his medical bag, he takes a stomach tube with a rubber funnel at the end. Then he starts to lift Fran off the bed.

DR. DREYFUSS: Help me, will you?

Between them, they get Fran into an upright position.

DR. DREYFUSS: Into the bathroom.

They half-carry, half-drag Fran's limp form toward the bathroom.

BUD: What are you going to do, Doc?

DR. DREYFUSS: Get that stuff out of her stomach – if it isn't too late. You better put some coffee on – and pray.

Bud starts away as Dr. Dreyfuss takes Fran into the bathroom.

Bud loses no time getting into the kitchen. He fills an aluminum kettle with water, strikes a match, lights the gas burner, puts the kettle on. Then he takes a jar of instant coffee and a chipped coffee mug out of the cupboard, shakes an excessive portion of coffee into the mug, sticks a spoon in it. He watches the kettle for a moment, mops his brow with a handkerchief, then starts back toward the bedroom.

Bud crosses the bedroom to the half-open door of the bathroom, looks in anxiously. From inside come the sounds of a coughing spasm and running water. Bud turns away, undoes his tie and collar, paces the bedroom floor. Something on the night table attracts his attention – resting against the base of the lamp is a sealed envelope. Bud picks

65

it up – on it, in Fran's handwriting, is one word, *JEFF. He turns the letter over in his hand, trying to decide what to do with it.*

Dr. Dreyfuss emerges from the bathroom, carrying a pale, still unconscious Fran. Bud quickly conceals the suicide note behind his back.

DR. DREYFUSS: Bring my bag.

He lugs Fran into the living room. Bud stashes the letter in his back pocket, picks up the medical bag, follows them.

In the living room, Dr. Dreyfuss lowers Fran into a chair. Her chin falls to her chest. Dreyfuss takes the bag from Bud, fishes out a hypodermic syringe, draws 2 c.c.'s from a bottle of picrotoxin.

DR. DREYFUSS: Roll up her right sleeve.

Bud does so. Dr. Dreyfuss hands the hypodermic to Bud, searches for a spot for the injection.

DR. DREYFUSS: Nice veins.

He swabs the spot with alcohol, takes the hypodermic back from Bud.

DR. DREYFUSS: Want to tell me what happended?

BUD: I don't know – I mean – I wasn't here – you see – we had some words earlier – nothing serious, really – what you might call a lovers' quarrel –

DR. DREYFUSS (*making off-scene injection*): So you went right out and picked yourself up

another dame.

BUD: Something like that.

DR. DREYFUSS: You know, Baxter, you're a real cutie-pie – yes, you are.

Bud just stands there, taking it. Fran stirs slightly, and from her parched lips comes a low moan. Dr. Dreyfuss grabs her by the hair, lifts her head up.

DR. DREYFUSS: If you'd come home half an hour later, you would have had quite a Christmas present.

With his free hand, Dr. Dreyfuss slaps Fran viciously across the face. Bud winces. Dreyfuss,

still holding Fran by the hair, takes a box of ammonia ampules out of his bag. He crushes one of the ampules in his hand, passes it under her nose. Fran tries to turn her head away. Dreyfuss slaps her again, hard, crushes another ampule, repeats the process.

Bud is watching tensely. From the kitchen comes the whistle of the boiling kettle, but Bud pays no attention.

DR. DREYFUSS: Get the coffee.

Bud hurries into the kitchen. He turns off the gas, pours the boiling water into the mug with the instant coffee, stirs it. From off, come the sounds of more

slapping and some moaning. Bud carries the coffee out.

In the living room, Dr. Dreyfuss is working another ammonia ampule under Fran's nose. Her eyes start fluttering. Dreyfuss takes the coffee mug from Bud, forces it between Fran's lips, pours coffee into her mouth. Fran resists instinctively, half the coffee dribbling over her chin and dress, but Dr. Dreyfuss keeps at it.

DR. DREYFUSS: Let's get some air in here. Open the windows.

Bud complies promptly – pulls up the shades, opens the windows wide.

DR. DREYFUSS (putting the empty mug down): What's her name?

BUD: Miss Kubelik – Fran.

DR. DREYFUSS (to Fran, slowly): Fran, I'm a doctor. I'm here because you took too many sleeping pills. Do you understand what I'm saying? (Fran mutters something) Fran, I'm Dr.

Dreyfuss – I'm here to help you. You took all those sleeping pills – remember?

FRAN (*mumbling groggily*): Sleeping pills.

DR. DREYFUSS: That's right, Fran. And I'm a doctor.

FRAN: Doctor.

DR. DREYFUSS: Dr. Dreyfuss.

FRAN: Dreyfuss.

DR. DREYFUSS (*to Bud*): Get more coffee.

Bud picks up the mug, leaves.

DR. DREYFUSS (*to Fran*): Tell me again – what's my name?

FRAN: Dr. Dreyfuss.

DR. DREYFUSS: And what happened to you?

FRAN: I took sleeping pills.

DR. DREYFUSS: Do you know where you are, Fran?

FRAN (*looking around blankly*): No.

DR. DREYFUSS: Yes, you do. Now concentrate.

FRAN: I don't know.

Bud is coming back with the coffee.

DR. DREYFUSS (*pointing to Bud*): Do you know who this is? (*Fran tries to focus*) Look at him.

FRAN: Mr. Baxter – nineteenth floor.

BUD: Hello, Miss Kubelik.

DR. DREYFUSS (*to Bud*): Mister – Miss – such politeness!

BUD (*to Dr. Dreyfuss, discreetly*): Well – we work in the same building – and we try to keep it quiet –

FRAN (*to Bud, puzzled*): What are you doing here?

Bud throws Dr. Dreyfuss a look, as if to say that Fran's mind still wasn't functioning properly.

BUD (*to Fran*): Don't you remember? We were at the office party together –

FRAN: Oh, yes – office party – Miss Olsen –

BUD: That's right. (*to Dr. Dreyfuss; improvising rapidly*) I told you we had a fight – that's what it was about – Miss Olsen – you know – that other girl you saw –

FRAN (*still trying to figure out Bud's presence*): I don't understand –

BUD: It's not important, Fran – the main thing is that I got here in time – and you're going to be all right – (*to Dr. Dreyfuss*) – isn't she, Doc?

FRAN (*closing her eyes*): I'm so tired –

DR. DREYFUSS: Here – drink this.

He forces her to swallow some coffee.

FRAN (*pushing the mug away*): Please – just let me sleep.

DR. DREYFUSS: You can't sleep. (*shaking her*) Come on, Fran – open your eyes. (*to Bud*) Let's get her walking. We've got to keep her awake for the next couple of hours.

They lift her from the chair, and each draping one of her arms over his shoulder, they start to walk her up and down the room.

DR. DREYFUSS (*urging Fran on*): Now walk, Fran. One, two, three, four – one, two, three, four – that's the idea – left, right, left, right – now we turn – one, two, three, four –

At first, Fran's feet just drag along the floor

between them. But gradually, as Dr. Dreyfuss'
voice continues droning hypnotically, she falls into
the rhythm of it, repeating the words after him and
putting her weight on her feet.

DR. DREYFUSS: Left, right, left, right – walk,
walk, walk – one, two, three, four – turn – left,
right, left, right – now you got it –

DISSOLVE TO:

95 INT. THE APARTMENT –
    DAWN

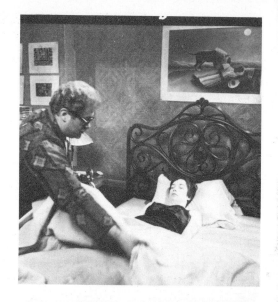

Through the bedroom window comes the first
faint light of dawn. Fran has been put to bed
by an exhausted Dr. Dreyfuss. She is in her slip,
and Dreyfuss is just drawing the blanket over her.
Her eyes are closed, and she is moaning fitfully.
Watching from the doorway is Bud, in shirt-
sleeves now, weary and dishevelled.

DR. DREYFUSS: She'll sleep on and off for the
next twenty-four hours. Of course, she'll
have a dandy hangover when she wakes up –

BUD: Just as long as she's okay.

DR. DREYFUSS (*massaging his calves*): These
cases are harder on the doctor than on the
patient. I ought to charge you by the mile.

They have now moved out into the living room,
where the overhead light and the Christmas tree
bulbs are still on.

DR. DREYFUSS: Any of that coffee left?

BUD: Sure.

He goes into the kitchen. Dr. Dreyfuss takes a
small notebook with a fountain pen clipped to it
out of his bag, sinks down on the couch.

DR. DREYFUSS: How do you spell her last
name?

BUD (*from kitchen*): Kubelik – with two k's.

DR. DREYFUSS: What's her address? (*no
answer from Bud*) Where does she live?

Bud appears from the kitchen, stirring the coffee
powder in a cup of hot water.

BUD (*apprehensive*): Why do you want to know,
Doc? You don't have to report this, do you?

DR. DREYFUSS: It's regulations.

BUD (*setting the coffee down*): She didn't mean it, Doc – it was an accident – she had a little too much to drink and – she didn't know what she was doing – there was no suicide note or anything – believe me, Doc, I'm not thinking about myself –

DR. DREYFUSS (*sipping the hot coffee*): Aren't you?

BUD: It's just that she's got a family – and there's the people in the office – look, Doc,

72

can't you forget you're a doctor – let's just say you're here as a neighbor –

DR. DREYFUSS (*a long look at Bud*): Well, as a doctor, I guess I can't prove it *wasn't* an accident. (*closes notebook*) But as your neighbor, I'd like to kick your keester clear around the block. (*indicating coffee*) Mind if I cool this off? *He uncaps the bottle of Scotch, pours a large slug into his coffee.*

BUD: Help yourself.

Dr. Dreyfuss (*taking a big gulp of the spiked coffee*): I don't know what you did to that girl in there – and don't tell me – but it was bound to happen, the way you carry on. Live now, pay later. Diner's Club! (*another swig*) Why don't you grow up, Baxter? Be a *mensch*! You know what that means?

Bud: I'm not sure.

Dr. Dreyfuss: A mensch – a human being! So you got off easy this time – so you were lucky –

Bud: Yeah, wasn't I?

Dr. Dreyfuss (*finishing coffee*): But you're not out of the woods yet, Baxter – because most of them try it again! (*picks up bag, starts toward door*) You know where I am if you need me.

He walks out, closing the door after him. Bud dejectedly turns off the overhead light, kicks out the plug of the Christmas tree lights, trudges into the bedroom.

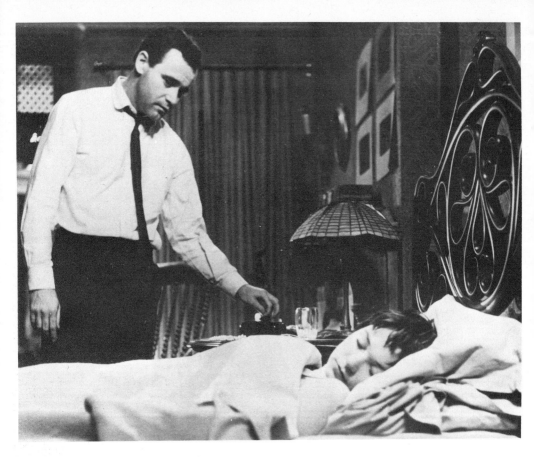

Fran is fast asleep. Bud picks up her dress, gets a hanger, drapes the dress over it, hangs it from the door. An early morning chill has invaded the room, and Bud switches on the electric blanket to keep Fran warm. Then he slumps into a chair beside the bed, looks at Fran compassionately. The light on the dial of the electric blanket glows in the grayish room. Bud just sits there, watching Fran.

FADE OUT:

FADE IN:

96 INT. STAIRCASE – BROWNSTONE HOUSE – DAY

Mrs. Lieberman, followed by her dog, is climbing the stairs to Bud's apartment, puffing asthmatically. She seems quite angry as she arrives at the door and rings the bell. There is no answer. She starts knocking impatiently.

MRS. LIEBERMAN: Mr. Baxter. Open up already!

Finally the door opens a crack, and Bud peers out. He looks like a man who has slept in his clothes – rumpled, bleary-eyed, unshaven.

BUD: Oh – Mrs. Lieberman.

MRS. LIEBERMAN: So who did you think it was – Kris Kringle? What was going on here last night?

BUD: Last night?

MRS. LIEBERMAN: All that marching – tramp, tramp, tramp – you were having army maneuvers maybe?

BUD: I'm sorry, Mrs. Lieberman – I'll never invite those people again.

MRS. LIEBERMAN: What you get from renting to bachelors. All night I didn't sleep ten minutes – and I'm sure you woke up Dr. Dreyfuss.

BUD: Don't worry about Dr. Dreyfuss – I happen to know he was out on a case.

MRS. LIEBERMAN: I'm warning you, Mr. Baxter – this is a respectable house, not a honky-tonky. (*to the dog*) Come on, Oscar.

Bud watches her start down the stairs with the dog, withdraws into the apartment.

97   INT. THE APARTMENT – DAY

Bud closes the door, crosses toward the bedroom, looks inside. Fran is asleep under the electric blanket, breathing evenly. He tries to shut the bedroom door, but it won't close completely because Fran's dress, on a hanger, is hooked over the top. He goes to the phone, picks it up, dials the operator.

BUD (*his voice low*): Operator, I want White Plains, New York – Mr. J. D. Sheldrake – (*an added thought*) – make it person to person.

98   INT. LIVING ROOM – SHELDRAKE HOUSE – DAY

The décor is split-level Early American. There is a huge Christmas tree and a jumble of presents, open gift boxes, and discarded wrappings.

Sheldrake and his two sons, TOMMY *and* JEFF JR., *are squatting on the floor, testing a Cape Canaveral set the kids got for Christmas.*

Sheldrake is in a brand new dressing gown, with a manufacturer's tag still dangling from it, and the boys are in pajamas and astronaut's helmets. As for the Cape Canaveral set, it is a miniature layout of block-houses, launching pads, and assorted space-missiles. Tommy has his finger on the button controlling one of the rockets.

SHELDRAKE (*counting down*): 7-6-5-4-3-2-1 – let her rip!

Tommy presses the button, and a spring sends the rocket toward the ceiling. Just then, the phone in the entrance hall starts ringing.

JEFF JR.: I'll get it.

He hurries to the phone.

TOMMY: Hey, Dad – why don't we put a fly in the nose cone and see if we can bring it back alive?

SHELDRAKE: It's a thought.

TOMMY: Maybe we should send up *two* flies – and see if they'll propagate in orbit.

SHELDRAKE: See if they'll *what*?

TOMMY: Propagate – you know, multiply – baby flies?

SHELDRAKE: Oh – *oh*!

JEFF JR. (*coming back from the phone*): It's for you, Dad. A Mr. Baxter.

SHELDRAKE (*getting up*): Baxter?

JEFF JR.: Person to person.

Sheldrake heads quickly for the phone.

TOMMY (*to Jeff Jr.*): Come on – help me round up some flies.

In the entrance hall, Sheldrake picks up the phone, turns his back toward the living room, speaks in a low voice.

SHELDRAKE: Hello? – yes – what's on your mind, Baxter?

99   BUD – ON PHONE

BUD: I hate to disturb you, but something came up – it's rather important – and I think it would be a good idea if you could see me – at the apartment – as soon as possible.

100   SHELDRAKE – ON PHONE

SHELDRAKE: You're not making sense, Baxter. What's this all about?

101   BUD – ON PHONE

BUD: I didn't want to tell you over the phone – but that certain party – you know who I mean – I found her here last night – she had taken an overdose of sleeping pills.

102   SHELDRAKE – ON PHONE

SHELDRAKE: *What?*

From the stairway beyond him comes:

MRS. SHELDRAKE'S VOICE: What is it, Jeff? Who's on the phone?

Sheldrake turns from the phone. Halfway down the stairs is Mrs. Sheldrake, in a quilted house-robe.

SHELDRAKE (*a nice recovery*): One of our employees had an accident – I don't know why they bother me with these things on Christmas Day. (*into phone*) Yes, Baxter – just how serious is it?

Out of the corner of his eye, he watches Mrs. Sheldrake come down the stairs, pass behind him on the way to the living room.

103   BUD – ON PHONE

BUD: Well, it was touch and go there for a while – but she's sleeping it off now.

He glances through the half-open door toward the sleeping Fran.

BUD: I thought maybe you'd like to be here when she wakes up.

104   SHELDRAKE – ON PHONE

SHELDRAKE: That's impossible. (*an apprehensive look toward the living room*) You'll have to handle this situation yourself – as a matter of fact, I'm counting on you –

105   INT. THE APARTMENT – DAY

BUD (*into phone*): Yes, sir – I understand. (*taking Fran's letter out of his pocket*) She left a note – you want me to open it and read it to you? (*a beat*) Well, it was just a suggestion – no, you don't have to worry about that, Mr. Sheldrake – I kept your name out of it – so there'll be no trouble, police-wise or newspaper-wise –

As Bud continues talking on the phone, Fran, in the bedroom, opens her eyes, looks around vaguely, trying to figure out where she is. She sits up in bed, winces, holds her head in her hands – she has a fierce hangover.

BUD (*into phone*): – you see, the doctor, he's a

friend of mine – we were very lucky in that respect – actually, he thinks she's my girl – no, he just jumped to the conclusion – around here, I'm known as quite a ladies' man –

In the bedroom Fran, becoming aware of Bud's voice, crawls out of bed and holding on to the furniture, moves unsteadily toward the living room door.

BUD (*into phone*): – of course, we're not out of the woods yet – sometimes they try it again – yes sir, I'll do my best – it looks like it'll be a couple of days before she's fully recovered, and I may have a little problem with the landlady –

Behind him, Fran appears in the bedroom doorway, barefooted and in her slip. She leans groggily against the door post, trying to focus on Bud and to concentrate on what he's saying.

BUD (*into phone*): – all right, Mr. Sheldrake, I'll keep her in my apartment as long as I can – any sort of message you want me to give her? – well, I'll think of something – goodbye, Mr. Sheldrake.

He hangs up the phone slowly.

FRAN (*weakly*): I'm sorry.

Bud turns around, sees her standing there on rubbery legs.

FRAN: I'm sorry, Mr. Baxter.

BUD: Miss Kubelik – (*he hurries toward her*) – you shouldn't be out of bed.

FRAN: I didn't know – I had no idea this was your apartment –

BUD (*putting his arm around her*): Let me help you.

He leads her back into the bedroom.

FRAN: I'm so ashamed. Why didn't you just let me die?

BUD: What kind of talk is that? (*he lowers her onto the bed*) So you got a little over-emotional – but you're fine now.

FRAN (*a groan*): My head – it feels like a big wad of chewing gum. What time is it?

BUD: Two o'clock.

FRAN (*struggling to her feet*): Where's my dress?

I have to go home.

Her knees buckle. Bud catches her.

BUD: You're in no condition to go anywhere – except back to bed.

FRAN: You don't want me·here –

BUD: Sure I do. It's always nice to have company for Christmas.

He tries to put her back to bed. Fran resists.

BUD: Miss Kubelik, I'm stronger than you are –

FRAN: I just want to go brush my teeth –

BUD: Oh – of course. I think there's a new toothbrush somewhere.

He crosses to the bathroom, takes a plaid robe off the hook on the back of the door, hands it to Fran.

BUD: Here – put this on.

In the bathroom, he finds an unused toothbrush in a plastic container. His eyes fall on his safety razor. With a glance toward the bedroom, he unscrews the razor, removes the blade, drops it in his shirt pocket. Then he empties the blades from the dis-

Mrs Dreyfuss opens the door.

BUD: Mrs. Dreyfuss, can I borrow some coffee
– and maybe an orange and a couple of eggs?

MRS. DREYFUSS (*contemptuously*): Eggs he asks
me for. Oranges. What you need is a good
horse-whipping.

BUD: Ma'am?

MRS. DREYFUSS: From me the doctor has no
secrets. Poor girl – how could you do a thing
like that?

BUD: I didn't really do anything – honest – I
mean, you take a girl out a couple of times a
week – just for laughs – and right away she
thinks you're serious – marriage-wise.

MRS. DREYFUSS: Big shot! For you, I wouldn't
lift a finger – but for her, I'll fix a little something to eat.

*She slams the door in his face. Bud starts back to
his apartment.*

107   INT. THE APARTMENT – DAY

*Fran enters shakily from the bedroom, looks
around for the phone, locates it, picks it up. As
she starts dialling, Bud comes in from the hall.*

BUD: Who are you calling, Miss Kubelik?

FRAN: My sister – she'll want to know what
happened to me.

BUD (*alarmed*): Wait a minute – let's talk this
over first. (*hurries up to her, takes the receiver
away*) Just what are you going to tell her?

FRAN: Well, I haven't figured it out, exactly.

BUD: You better figure it out – exactly. Suppose she asks you why you didn't come home
last night?

FRAN: I'll tell her I spent the night with a
friend.

BUD: Who?

FRAN: Someone from the office.

BUD: And where are you now?

FRAN: In his apartment.

BUD: *His* apartment?

FRAN: I mean – *her* apartment.

BUD: What's your friend's name?

*penser, puts those in his pocket. Now he notices a
bottle of iodine on the medicine shelf, stashes that
in another pocket, just as Fran appears in the
doorway wearing the robe.*

BUD (*handing her the toothbrush*): Here. How
about some breakfast?

FRAN: No – I don't want anything.

BUD: I'll fix you some coffee.

*He crosses the bedroom, heading for the kitchen,
stops.*

BUD: Oh – we're all out of coffee – you had
quite a lot of it last night –

*He thinks for a moment, hurries toward the hall
door.*

106   INT. SECOND FLOOR LANDING –
DAY

*Bud comes out of his apartment, leaving the door
half open, heads for the Dreyfuss apartment. He
rings the bell, peers down over the banister to
make sure Mrs. Lieberman isn't snooping around.*

FRAN: Baxter.

BUD: What's her first name?

FRAN: Miss. (*she is impressed with her own cleverness*)

BUD: When are you coming home?

FRAN: As soon as I can walk.

BUD: Something wrong with your legs?

FRAN: No – it's my stomach.

BUD: Your stomach?

FRAN: They had to pump it out.

BUD (*hanging up the phone*): Miss Kubelik, I don't think you ought to call anybody – not till that chewing gum is out of your head. (*leads her into bedroom*)

FRAN: But they'll be worried about me – my brother-in-law may be calling the police –

BUD: That's why we have to be careful – we don't want to involve anybody – after all, Mr. Sheldrake is a married man –

FRAN: Thanks for reminding me.

She pulls away from him, starts to get into bed.

BUD (*contritely*): I didn't mean it that way – I was just talking to him on the phone – he's very concerned about you.

FRAN: He doesn't give a damn about me.

BUD: Oh, you're wrong. He told me –

FRAN: He's a liar. But that's not the worst part of it – the worst part is – I still love him.

The doorbell rings.

BUD: Must be Mrs. Dreyfuss – (*starts into living room*) – remember the doctor – from last night – that's his wife.

He opens the hall door. Mrs. Dreyfuss brushes past him with a tray full of food.

MRS. DREYFUSS: So where is the victim? (*Bud indicates the bedroom*) Max the Knife!

She sweeps into the bedroom, Bud tagging along.

MRS. DREYFUSS (*to Fran*): Nu, little lady, how are we feeling today?

FRAN: I don't know – kind of dizzy.

MRS. DREYFUSS: Here. The best thing for dizzy is a little noodle soup with chicken – white meat – and a glass of tea.

She sets the tray down on Fran's lap.

FRAN: Thank you. I'm really not hungry.

MRS. DREYFUSS: Go ahead! Eat! Enjoy!

She hands her the soup spoon, turns to Bud.

MRS. DREYFUSS: You wouldn't have such a thing as a napkin, would you?

BUD: Well, I have some paper towels –

MRS. DREYFUSS: Beatnik! Go to my kitchen – third drawer, under the good silver, there is napkins.

BUD: Yes, Mrs. Dreyfuss.

He starts out with a worried backward glance toward the two. Fran is just sitting there, the spoon in her hand, not touching the soup.

MRS. DREYFUSS: So what are you waiting for – a singing commercial?

FRAN: I can't eat.

Mrs. Dreyfuss takes the spoon from her, starts to feed her.

MRS. DREYFUSS: You *must* eat – and you must

get healthy – and you must forget him. Such a fine boy he seemed when he first moved in here – clean and cut – a regular Ivy Leaguer. Turns out he is King Farouk. Mit the drinking – mit the cha cha – mit the no napkins. A girl like you, for the rest of your life you want to cry in your noodle soup? Who needs it! You listen to me, you find yourself a nice, substantial man – a widower maybe – and settle down – instead of nashing all those sleeping pills – for what, for whom? – for some Good Time Charlie? (*sees Bud approaching with napkin*) Sssh!

BUD (*gaily*): One napkin, coming up. (*hands it to Fran*) I wish we had some champagne to wrap it around.

MRS. DREYFUSS (*to Fran*): What did I tell you?

BUD (*uncomfortable*): Look, Mrs. Dreyfuss, you don't have to wait around. I'll wash the dishes and –

MRS. DREYFUSS: You wash 'em, you break 'em. I'll come back for them later. (*to Fran*) If he makes trouble, give me a yell.

She exits.

FRAN: She doesn't seem to like you very much.

BUD: Oh, I don't mind. As a matter of fact, I'm sort of flattered – that anybody should think a girl like you – would do a thing like this – over a guy like me.

FRAN (*glancing at night table*): Oh. Did you find something here – an envelope – ?

BUD: Yes, I've got it. (*takes envelope out of back pocket*) Don't you think we'd better destroy it? So it won't fall into the wrong hands – ?

FRAN: Open it.

Bud tears open the envelope, takes out Sheldrake's hundred dollars.

BUD: There's nothing here but a hundred dollar bill.

FRAN: That's right. Will you see that Mr. Sheldrake gets it?

BUD (*shrugging*): Sure.

He puts the money in his pocket.

FRAN (*holding out tray*): Here – take this, will you?

Bud relieves her of the tray, sets it down.

BUD: You want me to move the television set in here? (*Fran shakes her head*) You play gin rummy?

FRAN: I'm not very good at it.

BUD: I am. Let me get the cards.

FRAN: You don't have to entertain me.

Bud opens the bureau drawer, takes out a deck of cards, a score pad, and a pencil.

BUD: Nothing I'd like better – you know, togetherness. Guess what I did last Christmas. Had an early dinner at the automat, then went to the zoo, then I came home and cleaned up after Mr. Eichelberger – he had a little eggnog

party here. I'm way ahead this year.

He pulls a chair up to the bed, starts to shuffle the cards.

BUD: Three across, spades double, high deals. (*they cut*) Eight – ten. (*he starts to deal*)

FRAN (*pensively*): I think I'm going to give it all up.

BUD: Give what up?

FRAN: Why do people have to love people, anyway?

BUD: Yeah – I know what you mean. (*flips over down card*) Queen.

FRAN: I don't want it.

BUD: Pick a card.

She does, and they start playing.

FRAN: What do you call it when somebody keeps getting smashed up in automobile accidents?

BUD: A bad insurance risk?

FRAN (*nodding*): That's me with men. I've been jinxed from the word go – first time I was ever kissed was in a cemetery.

BUD: A cemetery?

FRAN: I was fifteen – we used to go there to smoke. His name was George – he threw me over for a drum majorette.

BUD: Gin.

He spreads his hand. Fran lays her cards down, and Bud adds them up.

BUD: Thirty-six and twenty-five – that's sixty-one and two boxes. (*enters score on pad*)

FRAN: I just have this talent for falling in love with the wrong guy in the wrong place at the wrong time.

BUD (*shuffling*): How many guys were there?

FRAN (*holding up four fingers*): Three. The last one was manager of a finance company, back home in Pittsburgh – they found a little shortage in his accounts, but he asked me to wait for him – he'll be out in 1965.

BUD (*pushing the deck toward her*): Cut.

FRAN (*she does, and he starts dealing*): So I came to New York and moved in with my sister and her husband – he drives a cab. They sent me to secretarial school, and I applied for a job with Consolidated – but I flunked the typing test –

BUD: Too slow?

FRAN: Oh, I can type up a storm, but I can't spell. So they gave me a pair of white gloves and stuck me in an elevator – that's how I met Jeff – (*her eyes mist up, and she puts her cards down*) Oh, God, I'm so fouled up. What am I going to do now?

BUD: You better win a hand – you're on a blitz.

FRAN: Was he really upset when you told him?

BUD: Mr. Sheldrake? Oh, yes. Very.

FRAN: Maybe he *does* love me – only he doesn't have the nerve to tell his wife.

BUD: I'm sure that's the explanation.

FRAN: You really think so?

BUD: No doubt about it.

FRAN: (*a thoughtful beat, then*): Can I have that pad and the pencil?

BUD (*handing her score pad and pencil*): What for?

FRAN: I'm going to write a letter to *Mrs.* Sheldrake.

BUD: You *are?*

FRAN: As one woman to another – I'm sure she'll understand –

BUD: Miss Kubelik, I don't think that's such a good idea.

He gently takes the pad and pencil away from her.

FRAN: Why not?

BUD: Well, for one thing, you can't spell. And secondly – if you did something like that – you'd hate yourself.

FRAN (*fighting back tears*): I don't like myself very much anyway.

BUD: Pick up your cards and let's go.

FRAN: Do I have to?

BUD: You bet. I got a terrific hand.

Fran, her eyes drooping sleepily, picks up her cards, makes a discard.

BUD: You sure you want to throw that card?

FRAN: Sure.

BUD: Gin.

He removes the cards from her hand, starts to add them up.

BUD: Fifty-two and twenty-five – that's seventy-seven – spades is double – a hundred and fifty-four – and four boxes – you're blitzed in two games.

He enters the score on the pad. As he starts to shuffle again, he notices that Fran has slid down on the pillow, and that her eyes are closed – she is asleep.

Bud rises, adjusts the blanket over her. He stands there looking at her for a moment, runs his hand over his chin. Realizing he needs a shave, he crosses to the bathroom.

In the bathroom, Bud washes his face, squirts some shaving cream into his hand, starts to apply it.

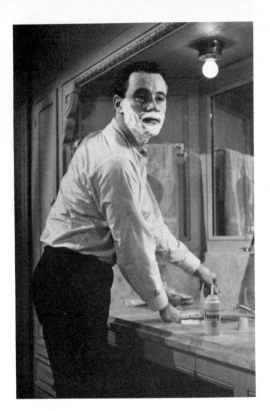

his face when the doorbell rings. He starts into the bedroom.

BUD (*muttering to himself*): All right – all right, Mrs. Dreyfuss.

He glances at the sleeping Fran, picks up the tray, carries it into the living room, pulling the bedroom door closed behind him. But it doesn't shut completely, because of Fran's dress hooked over the top.

Bud crosses to the hall door, opens it. Outside are Kirkeby, with the champagne bucket, and Sylvia.

KIRKEBY: Hi, Baxter.

BUD (*blocking the door*): What do you want?

KIRKEBY: What do I – ? (*to Sylvia*) Just a minute.

He pushes his way into the apartment past Bud.

BUD: You can't come in.

KIRKEBY (*closing the door behind him*): What's the matter with you, Buddy-boy? I made a reservation for four o'clock, remember?

He heads for the coffee table, sets the champagne down. Bud shoots a quick glance toward the bedroom door, gets rid of the tray.

BUD: Look, you can't stay here. Just take your champagne and go.

KIRKEBY: Baxter, I don't want to pull rank on you – but I told the lady it was all set – you want to make a liar out of me?

BUD: Are you going to leave, Mr. Kirkeby, or do I have to throw you out?

As Bud spins him around, Kirkeby notices the dress on the bedroom door.

KIRKEBY: Buddy-boy, why didn't you say so? (*indicating dress*) You got yourself a little playmate, huh?

BUD: Now will you get out?

108   EXT. BROWNSTONE HOUSE – DAY

A Volkswagen draws up to the curb in front of the house. Kirkeby gets out on the street side, Sylvia squeezes herself out through the other door. Kirkeby raises the front hood of the Volkswagen, reaches into the luggage compartment, takes out a cardboard bucket with a bottle of champagne on ice. Together, he and Sylvia start up the steps of the house, Sylvia already cha cha-ing in anticipation.

109   INT. APARTMENT – DAY

In the bathroom, Bud has just finished lathering

110   INT. SECOND FLOOR LANDING – DAY

Outside the door of Bud's apartment, Sylvia is cha cha-ing impatiently. Up the stairs comes Dr. Dreyfuss, in his overcoat and carrying his medical bag.

SYLVIA (*knocking on the door*): Hey, come on, what are we waiting for? Open up, will you? *She continues cha cha-ing. Dr. Dreyfuss has unlocked the door to his apartment, and is watching Sylvia, appalled by the fact that Baxter seems to be at it again. He starts inside.*
DR. DREYFUSS (*calling*): Mildred – !
He shuts the door behind him.
SYLVIA (*knocking on Baxter's door*): What's holding things up?

111 INT. APARTMENT – DAY
Kirkeby looks toward the door in response to

Sylvia's knocking.

KIRKEBY: Say, why don't we have ourselves a party – the four of us ?

BUD: No!

He forces Kirkeby toward the hall door. Kirkeby, glancing past him through the partly-open door of the bedroom, catches sight of Fran asleep in bed.

KIRKEBY (*grinning smugly*): Well, I don't blame you. So you hit the jackpot, eh kid – I mean, Kubelik-wise ? (*Bud opens the door, gestures him out*) Don't worry. I won't say a word to anybody.

112   INT. SECOND FLOOR LANDING – DAY

Kirkeby comes backing out the door of Bud's apartment, minus the champagne bucket.

KIRKEBY: Stay with it, Buddy-boy! (*Bud shuts the door on him*) Come on, Sylvia.

SYLVIA: What gives ?

KIRKEBY: A little mixup in signals. Let's go.

SYLVIA: Go where ?

KIRKEBY (*leading her toward stairs*): What's your mother doing this afternoon ?

SYLVIA: She's home – stuffing a turkey.

KIRKEBY: Why don't we send her to a movie – like Ben-Hur ?

SYLVIA: That's fine. But what are we going to do about grandma and Uncle Herman and Aunt Sophie and my two nieces –

113   INT. APARTMENT – DAY

Bud comes into the bedroom. As he heads for the bathroom, Fran stirs slightly, opens her eyes.

FRAN: Who was that ?

BUD: Just somebody delivering a bottle of champagne. Like some ?

FRAN (*shaking her head*): Would you mind opening the window ?

She turns off the electric blanket as Bud crosses to the window, pushes it up. Then a thought strikes him, and he looks at Fran suspiciously.

BUD: Now don't go getting any ideas, Miss Kubelik.

FRAN: I just want some fresh air.

BUD: It's only one story down – the best you can do is break a leg.

FRAN: So they'll shoot me – like a horse.

BUD (*approaching the bed*): Please, Miss Kubelik, you got to promise me you won't do anything foolish.

FRAN: Who'd care ?

BUD: I would.

FRAN (*sleepily*): Why can't I ever fall in love with somebody nice like you ?

BUD (*ruefully*): Yeah. Well – that's the way it crumbles, cookie-wise. Go to sleep.

Fran closes her eyes. Bud returns to the bathroom, picks up his razor, starts to shave. But something seems to be wrong with the razor – and unscrewing it, he realizes that there is no blade. Sheepishly, he takes out the blade he hid in his shirt pocket, inserts it in his razor, screws it shut. Then he resumes shaving.   FADE OUT:

FADE IN:

114   INT. SHELDRAKE'S ANTEROOM – DAY

It is the morning after Christmas, and Miss Olsen and the other girls are just settling down to work. Sheldrake, in hat and coat, approaches from the elevators, comes through the glass doors.

SECRETARIES (*ad lib*): Good morning, Mr. Sheldrake.

SHELDRAKE (*ignoring them*): Miss Olsen, will you come into my office, please ?

He strides into the inner office. Miss Olsen picks up her stenographic pad, follows him in.

115   INT. SHELDRAKE'S OFFICE – DAY

Sheldrake is removing his hat and coat as Miss Olsen comes in, shuts the door behind her.

MISS OLSEN: Did you have a nice Christmas ?

SHELDRAKE: Lovely. You were a big help.

MISS OLSEN: Me ?

SHELDRAKE: Thank you for giving that little pep talk to Miss Kubelik at the office party.

MISS OLSEN (*dropping her business-like mask*): I'm sorry, Jeff. You know I could never hold my liquor –

SHELDRAKE: But I thought you could hold your tongue.

MISS OLSEN: It won't happen again.

SHELDRAKE: You bet it won't. I'll arrange for you to get a month's severance pay – (*she looks at him uncomprehending*) That's right, Miss Olsen, I'm letting you go.

MISS OLSEN (*quietly*): You let me go four years ago, Jeff. Only you were cruel enough to make me sit out there and watch the new models pass by.

SHELDRAKE: I'd appreciate it if you'd be out of here as soon as you can.

MISS OLSEN (*formal again*): Yes, Mr. Sheldrake. *She turns and walks out of the office, shutting the door. Sheldrake looks after her for a moment, then goes to his desk, picks up the phone, dials the operator.*

SHELDRAKE (*into phone*): This is Mr. Sheldrake. I'd like Mr. Baxter's home telephone number – that's C. C. Baxter, in Ordinary Premium Accounting –

116 INT. SHELDRAKE'S ANTEROOM – DAY

Miss Olsen has put on her coat, and is going through her desk drawers, cleaning out her personal belongings – nail polish, emery boards, an extra pair of glasses, etc. As she stows them away in her handbag, one of the buttons on the telephone lights up, Miss Olsen hesitates for a second, then with a quick look around, she pushes the button down, carefully picks up the receiver, listens in.

117 INT. SHELDRAKE'S OFFICE – DAY

Sheldrake is dialing the last two digits of a telephone number. After a moment, someone answers.

SHELDRAKE: Hello, Baxter? Jeff Sheldrake. Can you talk?

118 INT. THE APARTMENT – DAY

Bud, wearing slacks, a shirt open at the neck, and a cardigan sweater, is at the phone.
A pillow and a blanket on the living room couch indicate where he spent the night.

BUD (*looking off*): Yes, she's in the shower – she's coming along fine, considering.

119 SHELDRAKE – ON PHONE

SHELDRAKE: Good. Is there anything you need – money – ?

120 BUD – ON PHONE

BUD: No, thank you, Mr. Sheldrake. As a matter of fact, I've got some money for you – a hundred dollars –

121 SHELDRAKE – ON PHONE

SHELDRAKE: Oh. (*a beat*) Well, if there's anything I can do for you –

122 BUD – ON PHONE

BUD: For me? I don't think so. But I was hoping maybe you could do something for *her* –

123 SHELDRAKE – ON PHONE

SHELDRAKE: Like what? Put yourself in my place, Baxter – how can I help her – my hands are tied –

124 INT. APARTMENT – DAY

Fran now appears in the bedroom, wearing the plaid robe, and toweling her damp hair.

BUD (*into phone*): Well, at least you can talk to her – let me put her on – and please be gentle – *He puts the receiver down, crosses toward the bedroom door.*

BUD: There's a call for you –

FRAN (*approaching*): For me?

BUD: – Mr. Sheldrake.

FRAN: I don't want to talk to him.
BUD: I think you should. I have to run down to the grocery anyway – all that's left around here is one·frozen pizza – (*takes raincoat and old hat from hanger*) I'll be right back – okay?
Fran nods, watches him go out. Then she glances toward the phone, which is off the hook. Reluctantly she advances toward it, picks it up.
FRAN (*into phone*): Hello, Jeff. (*a long beat*) Yes, I'm all right.

125   SHELDRAKE – ON PHONE
SHELDRAKE: Fran, why did you do it? It's so childish – and it never solves anything – I ought to be very angry with you, scaring me like that – but let's forget the whole thing – pretend it never happened – what do you say, Fran? (*no answer*) Fran –

126   INT. SHELDRAKE'S ANTEROOM
Miss Olsen, glued to the phone, is listening intently.

127   SHELDRAKE – ON PHONE
SHELDRAKE: Are you there, Fran?

128   FRAN – ON PHONE
FRAN: Of course I'm not here – because the whole thing never happened – I never took those pills – I never loved you – we never even met – isn't that the way you want it?

129   SHELDRAKE – ON PHONE
SHELDRAKE: There you go again – you know I didn't mean it that way, Fran. Just get well – do what the nurse tells you – I mean Baxter – and I'll see you as soon as I can. 'Bye, Fran. (*he hangs up*)

130   INT. SHELDRAKE'S ANTEROOM – DAY
Miss Olsen hangs up the phone, sits there for a moment, weighing what she has overheard. Then
90

she makes a decision, picks up the phone again, dials a number. As she waits for an answer, she glances toward Sheldrake's office.
MISS OLSEN (*into phone*): Hello, Mrs. Sheldrake? This is Miss Olsen – fine, thank you – Mrs. Sheldrake, I was wondering if we could have lunch together? – well, I don't know how important it is, but I think you might find it educational – it concerns your husband – all right, one o'clock, at Longchamp's. Madison and 59th.
She looks up as the door to the inner office opens and Sheldrake comes out, He stops when he sees that Miss Olsen is still there.
MISS OLSEN (*hanging up phone*): Don't worry, I'm on my way. (*she rises*) I was just making a personal call.
She opens her handbag, takes out a coin, puts it down on the desk.
MISS OLSEN: Here's a dime.
She marches out through the glass doors toward the elevators as Sheldrake stands there, watching her.   DISSOLVE TO:

131   EXT. BROWNSTONE HOUSE – DAY
Bud comes down the street, carrying a large brown paper bag overflowing with groceries. He goes up the steps of the house and through the front door.

132   INT. STAIRCASE AND SECOND FLOOR LANDING – DAY
As Bud starts up the stairs, with the groceries, Mrs. Lieberman comes hurrying down toward him.
MRS. LIEBERMAN (*breathlessly*): Oh, Mr. Baxter – I'm glad you're here – I was going to get the passkey.
BUD: What for?
MRS. LIEBERMAN: I thought I smelled gas coming from your apartment.
BUD: *Gas?*
He races up the stairs two at a time, fumbling frantically for his key. Reaching the door of his

apartment, he unlocks it, dashes in.

133 INT. THE APARTMENT – DAY

Bud comes bursting through the door. The living room is empty, and the bedclothes have been removed from the couch.

BUD (*calling*): Miss Kubelik!

He dumps the bag of groceries on a table, rushes into the kitchen. The burner has been turned on under the kettle, but there is no flame, and gas is hissing from the vents. Bud snaps it off, starts out again.

BUD: Miss Kubelik!

Meanwhile Fran has appeared from the bathroom, and is approaching the bedroom door. She is still in her robe, and is holding a double sock-stretcher with one of Bud's socks on it. Bud, rounding the corner from the kitchen at full speed, collides with Fran in the bedroom doorway. He grabs her arms with obvious relief.

BUD: Are you all right?

FRAN: Sure. (*sniffs*) What's that funny smell?

BUD: Gas. (*indicating kitchen*) Didn't you turn it on?

FRAN: Yes. I was boiling some water to get the coffee stains out of my dress.

BUD (*accusingly*): You turned it on – but you didn't *light* it.

FRAN: Are you supposed to?

BUD: In *this* house, you're supposed to.

FRAN: Oh.

Bud starts to take off his hat and coat, notices the sock-stretcher in her hand.

BUD: What are you doing with that?

FRAN: I was washing my stockings, so I decided I might as well do your socks.

BUD: Thank you.

FRAN: It's very curious – I could only find three and a half pair.

BUD: Well, things are a little disorganized around here.

He carries the bag of groceries into the kitchen, Fran trailing after him. During the following, he removes the contents of the bag – bread, eggs, bacon, spaghetti, ground round, frankfurters and assorted canned goods – sets them out on the drainboard.

FRAN: I'd say. What's a tennis racquet doing in the kitchen?

She produces the racquet from behind the stove.

BUD: Tennis racquet? Oh, I remember – I was cooking myself an Italian dinner. (*Fran looks at him oddly*) I used it to strain the spaghetti.

FRAN: (*thinking it over*) Why not?

BUD: As a matter of fact, I'm a pretty good cook – but I'm a lousy housekeeper.

FRAN: Yes, you are. (*indicating the living room*) When I was straightening up the couch, you know what I found? Six hairpins, a lipstick, a pair of false eyelashes, and a swizzle stick from the Stork Club.

BUD (*shrugging*): It's just that I'm the kind of guy who can't say no – I don't mean to *girls* – I mean –

FRAN: You mean to someone like Mr. Sheldrake.

BUD: I guess so.

FRAN: I know so. He's a taker.

BUD: A what?

FRAN: Some people take, some people get took – and they know they're getting took – and there's nothing they can do about it.

BUD: I wouldn't say that – (*trying to change the subject*) What would you like to have for dinner? There's onion soup and canned asparagus –

FRAN: I really ought to be getting home. My family will be flipping by now.

She starts into the living room. Bud follows her.

BUD: You can't leave yet. The doctor says it takes forty-eight hours to get the stuff out of your system.

FRAN (*wistfully*): I wonder how long it takes to get someone you're stuck on out of your system? If they'd only invent some kind of a pump for that –

She sits on the arm of a chair.

BUD: I know how you feel, Miss Kubelik. You think it's the end of the world – but it's not, really. I went through exactly the same thing myself.

FRAN: You did?

BUD: Well, maybe not *exactly* – I tried to do it with a gun.

FRAN: Over a girl?

BUD: Worse than that – she was the wife of my best friend – and I was mad for her. But I knew it was hopeless – so I decided to end it all. I went to a pawnshop and bought a forty-five automatic and drove up to Eden Park – do you know Cincinnati?

FRAN: No, I don't.

BUD: Anyway, I parked the car and loaded the gun – well, you read in the papers all the time that people shoot themselves, but believe me, it's not that easy – I mean, how do you do it? – here, or here, or here – (*with cocked finger, he points to his temple, mouth and chest*) – you know where I finally shot myself?

FRAN: Where?

BUD (*indicating kneecap*): Here.

FRAN: In the knee?

BUD: Uh-huh. While I was sitting there, trying to make my mind up, a cop stuck his head in the car, because I was illegally parked – so I started to hide the gun under the seat and it went off – pow!

FRAN (*laughing*): That's terrible.

BUD: Yeah. Took me a year before I could bend my knee – but I got over the girl in three weeks. She still lives in Cincinnati, has four kids, gained twenty pounds – she sends me a fruit cake every Christmas.

FRAN (*suddenly suspicious*): Are you just making that up to make me feel better?

BUD: Of course not. Here's the fruit cake. (*shows it to her under Christmas tree*) And you want to see my knee? (*starts to raise pant-leg*)

FRAN: No, thanks. The fellows in the office may get the wrong idea how I found out.

BUD: So let 'em. Look, I'm going to cook dinner for us. We'll have the fruit cake for dessert. You just sit there and rest. You've done enough for one day.

FRAN (*smiling*): Yes, nurse.

Bud starts happily into the kitchen.

DISSOLVE TO:

134 INT. LOBBY INSURANCE BUILDING – DAY

It is mid-afternoon, and traffic is light. A Yellow Cab has pulled up in front of the entrance, and the driver, a stockily-built young man in a leather jacket and cap, gets out and comes through the revolving doors into the lobby. His name is KARL MATUSCHKA, *and he is Fran's brother-in-law. As he cases the elevators, the starter comes up to him.*

ELEVATOR STARTER: Can I help you?

MATUSCHKA: I'm looking for one of the elevator girls – Miss Kubelik.

ELEVATOR STARTER: So am I. She didn't report this morning.

MATUSCHKA: She didn't. Where can I get some information – who's in charge here?

ELEVATOR STARTER: That comes under General Office Administration. See Mr. Dobisch, twenty-first floor.

MATUSCHKA: Thanks.

He steps into an elevator, the doors of which are just closing.

135 INT. DOBISCH'S OFFICE – DAY

Dobisch is sitting behind his desk, lighting a cigar. Kirkeby, who has dropped in for a little visit, is perched on the edge of the desk.

KIRKEBY: – so yesterday afternoon I take Sylvia up to the apartment, and guess who he's got stashed away in the bedroom?

DOBISCH: Who?

KIRKEBY: Kubelik.

DOBISCH: No kidding. Buddy-boy and Kubelik having themselves a little toot!

KIRKEBY: Toot? It's more like a lost weekend. Neither of them showed up for work today.

DOBISCH: A.W.O.L.?

KIRKEBY: What gripes me is the two of them were guzzling my champagne while Sylvia and I wound up at the Guggenheim Museum.

The glass door opens and Matuschka comes in.

MATUSCHKA: Mr. Dobisch?

DOBISCH: Yeah.

MATUSCHKA: My name is Karl Matuschka – my sister-in-law, she runs one of the elevators here – Fran Kubelik.

KIRKEBY (*exchanging a glance with Dobisch*): Miss Kubelik?

MATUSCHKA: You know her?

DOBISCH: Of course. There may be a lot of employees here – but we're one big happy family.

MATUSCHKA: Well, she lives with us – and my wife, she's getting a little nervous – on account of Fran hasn't been home for two days.

KIRKEBY (*another look at Dobisch*): That so.

MATUSCHKA: Anyway, we was wondering if somebody in the office would know what happened to her.

DOBISCH: I see. (*to Kirkeby*) What do you think, Al? Can we help the man?

KIRKEBY (*after a pregnant pause*): Why not? We don't owe Buddy-boy anything.

DOBISCH: Yeah. What's Buddy-boy done for us lately?

MATUSCHKA (*scowling*): Who is Buddy-boy?

DISSOLVE TO:

136   INT. THE APARTMENT –
      EVENING

Buddy-boy is bending over a hot stove, preparing an Italian dinner. He takes a saucepan of spaghetti off the fire, and picking up the tennis racquet with the other hand, pours the spaghetti

on top of the racquet strings. Then he turns on the faucet, runs water over the spaghetti. With the combined technique of Brillat-Savarin and Pancho Gonzales, he gently agitates the racquet, letting the water drain off the spaghetti. As he works, he hums a theme from Tschaikowsky's Capriccio Italien.

Fran walks in, still in her robe.

FRAN: Are we dressing for dinner?

BUD: No – just come as you are.

FRAN (watching him): Say, you're pretty good with that racquet.

BUD: You ought to see my backhand. (dumping spaghetti into platter) And wait till I serve the meatballs. (demonstrates)

FRAN: Shall I light the candles?

BUD: It's a must – gracious-living-wise.

As Fran starts into the living room, Bud begins to ladle meat sauce onto the spaghetti, humming operatically.

In the living room, the small table has been set for two, and prominent on it is the champagne bottle that Mr. Kirkeby left behind, still in its cardboard bucket, but freshly iced. As Fran lights the candles, she notices the napkins on the table, peels a price-tag off the corner of one of them.

FRAN: I see you bought some napkins.

BUD: Might as well go all the way.

He carries the platter of spaghetti and meat sauce in from the kitchen, sets it on the table, sprinkles some cheese on it. Then he crosses to the coffee table, where a full martini pitcher stands in readiness, fills a couple of glasses. Fran seats

herself at the table.

BUD: You know, I used to live like Robinson Crusoe – shipwrecked among eight million people. Then one day I saw a footprint in the sand – and there you were – (*hands her martini*) It's a wonderful thing – dinner for two.

FRAN: You usually eat alone?

BUD: Oh, no. Sometimes I have dinner with Ed Sullivan, sometimes with Dinah Shore or Perry Como – the other night I had dinner with Mae West – of course, she was much younger then. (*toasting*) Cheers.

FRAN: Cheers.

They drink.

BUD: You know what we're going to do after dinner?

FRAN: The dishes?

BUD: I mean, after that?

FRAN: What?

BUD: You don't have to if you don't want to –

FRAN: I don't?

BUD: We're going to finish that gin game.

FRAN: Oh.

BUD: So I want you to keep a clear head.

The door bell rings. Carrying his martini glass, Bud crosses to the door, starts to open it.

BUD: Because I don't want to take advantage of you – the way I did yesterday in bed.

By now the door is open, and Bud is speaking to Fran over his shoulder He turns, finds himself face to face with Karl Matuschka, who is standing grimly in the doorway

MATUSCHKA: Baxter?

BUD: Yes?

Matuschka shoves him roughly aside, strides past him toward Fran, who has risen to her feet.

MATUSCHKA: What's with you, Fran – did you forget where you live?

FRAN (*to Bud*): This is my brother-in-law,

Karl Matuschka.

BUD (*friendly*): How do you do, Mr. Matuschka?

MATUSCHKA (*pushing Bud away; to Fran*): Okay, get your clothes on. I got the cab downstairs.

BUD: Now, wait a minute. I know what you're thinking – but it's not as bad as it looks –

MATUSCHKA (*shoving him away*): It's none of my business what you do, Fran – you're over twenty-one – but your sister happens to think you're a lady.

BUD: All we were going to do is eat and wash the dishes –

MATUSCHKA (*grabbing him*): Look, Buddy-boy – if there wasn't a lady present, I'd clobber you.

FRAN (*separating them*): All right, Karl – I'll get dressed.

She exits into the bedroom, removing her dress from the door, and closing it. Matuschka leans against the wall beside the hall door, eyeing Bud truculently. Bud raises a finger to remonstrate with him – then breaks into a nervous, ingratiating smile.

BUD.: Care for a martini? Champagne? (*Matuschka continues glaring at him*) How about a little spaghetti with meat sauce? Made it myself. (*Matuschka just scowls*) Your sister-in-law sure is terrific – (*realizes his mistake; switching abruptly*) Must be murder driving a cab in New York – I mean, with all that cross-town traffic –

He gestures with the martini glass, spilling the contents over his shirtfront. Through the partly open hall door, Dr. Dreyfuss sticks his head in.

DR. DREYFUSS: Hi, Baxter.

He steps into the apartment, passing Matuschka without seeing him.

DR. DREYFUSS: How's the patient?

BUD (*quickly*): Oh, I'm fine, Doc.

DR. DREYFUSS: Not you – Miss Kubelik.

MATUSCHKA (*stepping forward*): What's the matter with Miss Kubelik?

BUD: Oh, this is Mr. Matuschka – he's Miss

Kubelik's – he's got a cab downstairs –

MATUSCHKA (to Dreyfuss): Fran been sick or something?

Dr. Dreyfuss looks at Bud.

BUD: No, no – just had a little accident.

MATUSCHKA (*to Dreyfuss*): What does he mean, accident?

DR. DREYFUSS: Well, these things happen all the time –

MATUSCHKA: What things? (*grabbing Dreyfuss*) Say, what kind of doctor are you, anyway?

BUD (*hastily*): Oh, not that kind. He just gave her a shot and pumped her stomach out –

Behind them, the bedroom door has opened, and Fran comes out, wearing her coat over her dress.

MATUSCHKA: What for?

FRAN (*coming up*): Because I took some sleeping pills. But I'm all right now – so let's go.

MATUSCHKA: Why did you take sleeping pills?

BUD (*promptly*): On account of me.

MATUSCHKA (*whirling on him*): You?

BUD: Who else?

Matuschka lashes out with a left to Bud's jaw, and while he is off balance, catches him with a right to the eye. Bud falls back against the Christmas tree, which topples with a crash. Fran pulls Matuschka away from him.

FRAN: Leave him alone, Karl.

She kneels beside Bud.

FRAN (*tenderly*): You fool – you damn fool.

MATUSCHKA: Come on, Fran.

FRAN: Goodbye, Mr. Baxter.

She kisses him on the cheek, rises, starts toward the door.

FRAN: Goodbye, doctor.

She follows Matuschka out. Bud looks after her, starry-eyed.

DR. DREYFUSS: I don't want to gloat, but just between us, you had that coming to you. (*tilts Bud's chin up, examines his eye*) Tch, tch, tch. Are you going to have a shiner tomorrow. Let me get my bag. (*he starts out*)

BUD (*calling after him*): Don't bother, Doc. It

doesn't hurt a bit.
He is on Cloud Nine.   FADE OUT:

FADE IN:
137   INT. NINETEENTH FLOOR – DAY
Bud is coming from the elevators toward his office. He is wearing his chesterfield, bowler, and a pair of dark glasses. He opens the office door, starts in.

138   INT. BUD'S OFFICE – DAY
Bud crosses directly to the phone, removes his glasses – revealing a swollen left eye. He dials a

number.

BUD (*into phone*): Mr. Sheldrake's office? This is C. C. Baxter. Would you please tell Mr. Sheldrake I'd like to come up and see him? It's rather important. Will you call me back, please?
He hangs up, takes of his hat and coat, deposits them on the clothes-tree. Then he paces around the office, rehearsing a speech out loud.
BUD: Mr. Sheldrake, I've got good news for you. All your troubles are over. I'm going to take Miss Kubelik off your hands. (*nods to himself with satisfaction*) The plain fact is, Mr.

Sheldrake, that I love her. I haven't told her yet, but I thought you should be the first to know. After all, you don't really want her, and I do, and although it may sound presumptuous, she needs somebody like me. So I think it would be the thing all around – (*the phone rings and he picks it up*) – solution-wise. (*into phone*) Yes? I'll be right up.
He hangs up, crosses to the door, opens it.
BUD (*to himself*): Mr. Sheldrake, I've got good news for you –
Putting on his dark glasses, he heads for the elevators, still talking to himself.

139   INT. NINETEENTH FLOOR – DAY
Kirkeby and Dobisch are just stepping out of an elevator when Bud approaches. They grin smugly when they see that he is wearing dark glasses.
KIRKEBY: Hi, Buddy-boy. What happened to you?
DOBISCH: Hit by a swinging door? Or maybe a Yellow Cab?
Bud pays no attention, walks right past them into the elevator, still muttering to himself. The doors close.
KIRKEBY (*as they move away from the elevators*):

That guy really must've belted him.

DOBISCH: Yeah, he's punchy. Talking to himself.

140   INT. TWENTY-SEVENTH FLOOR FOYER – DAY

The elevator doors open.

ELEVATOR OPERATOR: Twenty-seven.

Bud steps out. As he heads for Sheldrake's office, he continues rehearsing his speech.

BUD: You see, Mr. Sheldrake, those two days she spent in the apartment – it made me realize how lonely I'd been before. But thanks to you,

I'm in a financial position to marry her – if I can ever square things with her family.

He opens the door to Sheldrake's anteroom.

141   INT. SHELDRAKE'S OFFICE – DAY

Sheldrake is pacing in front of his desk. A couple of suitcases are standing in a corner of the room. The intercom buzzes, and Sheldrake presses the lever down.

SECRETARY'S VOICE: Mr. Baxter is here.

SHELDRAKE: Send him in.

A beat, then the door opens, and Bud marches in determinedly.

BUD: Mr. Sheldrake, I've got good news for you –

SHELDRAKE: And I've got good news for you, Baxter. All your troubles are over.

BUD (*reacting to the echo*): Sir?

SHELDRAKE: I know how worried you were about Miss Kubelik – well, stop worrying – I'm going to take her off your hands.

BUD (*stunned*): *You're* going to take her off *my* hands?

SHELDRAKE: That's right. (*indicating suitcases*) I've moved out of my house – I'm going to be staying in town, at the Athletic Club.

BUD: You left your wife?

SHELDRAKE: Well, if you must know – I fired my secretary, my secretary got to my wife, and my wife fired me. Ain't that a kick in the head?

BUD: Yeah –

SHELDRAKE: Now what was your news, Baxter?

BUD (*recovering with difficulty*): It's about Miss Kubelik – she's all right again – so she went back home.

SHELDRAKE: Swell. And don't think I've forgotten what you did for me. (*opens door to adjoining office*) This way, Baxter.

Bud advances slowly toward the door.

142   INT. ADJOINING OFFICE – DAY

It is a slightly smaller and less lavish edition of

Sheldrake's office. Sheldrake ushers Bud through the door, points to the chair behind the desk.

SHELDRAKE: Sit down. Try it on for size.

Bud obeys like an automaton, lowers himself into the chair.

SHELDRAKE: You like? (*indicating office*) It's all yours.

BUD: Mine?

SHELDRAKE: My assistant, Roy Thompson, has been shifted to the Denver office, and you're taking his place. (*no reaction from Bud*) What's the matter, Baxter? You don't seem very excited.

BUD: Well, it's just that so many things have been happening so fast – I'm *very* pleased – especially for Miss Kubelik. Now that I've gotten to know her better, I think she's the kind of girl that definitely ought to be married to *somebody* –

SHELDRAKE: Oh, sure, sure. But first the property settlement has to be worked out – then it takes six weeks in Reno – meanwhile, I'm going to enjoy being a bachelor for a while. (*starts back toward his own office*) Oh, by the way, you can now have lunch in the executive dining room –

BUD: Yes, sir.

He removes his dark glasses reflectively.

SHELDRAKE: That's just one of the privileges that goes with this job. You also get a nice little expense account, the use of the executive washroom – (*breaks off, peers at Bud's face*) Say, what happened to you, Baxter?

BUD: I got kicked in the head, too.

SHELDRAKE: Oh?

With a shrug, he exits into his own office, closing the door behind him. Bud sits there, unconsciously bending the glasses in his hand until they suddenly snap in two. Bud glances down at the two broken halves, as though surprised by his own violence, tosses them on the desk.

DISSOLVE TO:

143   INT. LOBBY INSURANCE
         BUILDING – EVENING

We are close on the building directory. Listed under PERSONNEL *is* J. D. SHELDRAKE, *Director, and just below that a man's hand is inserting the name* C. C. BAXTER *in the slot marked Asst. Director. The lettering is complete except for the final R.*

Camera pulls back to reveal the sign painter we saw earlier, working on the directory. Watching him is Bud. He is wearing his chesterfield and bowler, and still has a slight welt under his left eye. It is after six o'clock, and there is very little activity in the lobby.

Fran, wearing her coat over street clothes, approaches from the direction of the elevators, stops when she sees Bud.

FRAN: Good evening, Mr. Baxter.

Bud turns to her in surprise, removes his bowler.

BUD: Oh, Miss Kubelik. How do you feel?

FRAN: Fine. How's your eye?

BUD: Fine.

There is a moment of constraint between them.

FRAN: How's everything at the apartment?

BUD: Nothing's changed. You know, we never finished that gin game –

FRAN: I know. (*a beat*) I suppose you heard about Mr. Sheldrake –?

BUD: You mean, leaving his wife? Yeah, I'm very happy for you.

FRAN: I never thought he'd do it.

BUD: I told you all along. You see, you were wrong about Mr. Sheldrake.

FRAN: I guess so.

BUD: For that matter, you were wrong about me, too. What you said about those who take and those who get took? Well, Mr. Sheldrake wasn't using me – I was using him. See? (*indicating his name on directory*) Last month I was at desk 861 on the nineteenth floor – now I'm on the twenty-seventh floor, panelled office, three windows – so it all worked out fine – we're both getting what we want.

FRAN: Yes. (*looks at her watch*) You walking to the subway?

BUD: No, thank you. (*fumbling*) I – well, to tell you the truth – (*glancing around lobby*) – I have this heavy date for tonight –

He points off toward the news-stand. Standing there is a tall attractive brunette, obviously waiting for someone. Fran looks off in the indicated direction.

FRAN: Oh.

BUD: Aren't you meeting Mr. Sheldrake?

FRAN: No. You know how people talk. So I decided it would be better if we didn't see each

other till everything is settled, divorce-wise.

BUD: That's very wise.

FRAN: Good night, Mr. Baxter.

BUD: Good night, Miss Kubelik.

Fran walks toward the revolving doors. Bud watches her for a moment, then strides briskly across the lobby toward the news-stand. He goes right past the waiting brunette, stops in front of a rack of pocket books, examines the merchandise. A man now comes out of a phone booth, joins the waiting brunette, and they go off together. Bud picks out a couple of paperbacks, pays the clerk behind the counter. Stuffing a book into each

coat pocket, he moves slowly toward the revolving
doors.   DISSOLVE TO:

144   INT. SHELDRAKE'S OFFICE – DAY
Sheldrake is swiveled around sideways behind his
desk, with a bootblack kneeling in front of him,
shining his shoes. Reaching for the intercom,
Sheldrake presses down one of the levers.
SHELDRAKE: Baxter – would you mind stepping
in here for a minute?
BAXTER'S VOICE: Yes. Mr. Sheldrake.
The bootblack finishes the second shoe with a
flourish, gathers up his equipment. Sheldrake

tosses him a half dollar.
BOOTBLACK: Much obliged.
He exits into the anteroom as the door of the
adjoining office opens and Bud comes in, carrying
several charts. There is no trace left of his black
eye.
BUD (*putting charts on desk*): Here's the break-
down of figures on personnel turnover. Thirty-
seven percent of our female employees leave to
get married, twenty-two percent quit because –
SHELDRAKE (*breaking in*): You're working too
hard, Baxter. It's New Year's Eve – relax.
BUD: Yes, sir.

SHELDRAKE: I suppose you'll be on the town tonight – celebrating?

BUD: Naturally.

SHELDRAKE: Me, too. I'm taking Miss Kubelik out – I finally talked her into it –

BUD: I see.

SHELDRAKE: The only thing is I'm staying at the Athletic Club – and it's strictly stag – so if you don't mind –

BUD: Don't mind what?

SHELDRAKE: You know that other key to your apartment – well, when we had that little scare about Miss Kubelik, I thought I'd better get rid of it quick – so I threw it out the window of the commuter train.

BUD: Very clever.

SHELDRAKE: Now I'll have to borrow your key.

BUD: Sorry, Mr. Sheldrake.

SHELDRAKE: What do you mean, sorry?

BUD: You're not going to bring anybody up to my apartment.

SHELDRAKE: I'm not just bringing *anybody* – I'm bringing Miss Kubelik.

BUD: *Especially* not Miss Kubelik.

SHELDRAKE: How's that again?

BUD (*flatly*): No key!

SHELDRAKE: Baxter, I picked you for my team because I thought you were a bright young man. You realize what you're doing? Not to me – but to yourself. Normally it takes years to work your way up to the twenty-seventh floor – but it takes only thirty seconds to be out on the street again. You dig?

BUD (*nodding slowly*): I dig.

SHELDRAKE: So what's it going to be?

Without taking his eyes off Sheldrake, Bud reaches into his pocket, fishes out a key, drops it on the desk.

SHELDRAKE: Now you're being bright?

BUD: Thank you, sir.

He turns abruptly, starts back into his own office.

145   INT. BUD'S NEW OFFICE – DAY

Bud comes in, shutting the door behind him, stands rooted to the spot for a moment. Then he takes some pencils out of his breast pocket and drops them into a container on the desk, closes his account book, slams a couple of open file drawers shut.

As he crosses to the clothes closet, the connecting door opens and Sheldrake comes in, key in hand.

SHELDRAKE: Say, Baxter – you gave me the

wrong key.

BUD: No I didn't.

SHELDRAKE (*holding it out*): But this is the key to the executive washroom.

BUD: That's right, Mr. Sheldrake. I won't be needing it – because I'm all washed up around here.

He has taken his chesterfield and bowler out of the closet, and is putting the coat on.

SHELDRAKE: What's gotten into you, Baxter?

BUD: Just following doctor's orders. I've decided to become a mensch. You know what that means? A human being.

SHELDRAKE: Now hold on, Baxter –

BUD: Save it. The old payola won't work any more. Goodbye, Mr. Sheldrake.

He opens the door to the anteroom, starts out.

146 INT. SHELDRAKE'S ANTEROOM – DAY

Bud comes out of his office, carrying his bowler, strides past the secretaries and through the glass doors to the foyer. An elevator is just unloading, and beside it a handyman is cleaning out one of the cigarette receptacles. Bud crosses to the elevator, and as he passes the handyman, he jams his bowler on the man's head – surrendering his crown, so to speak. The elevator doors close. The handyman straightens up, looks around in bewilderment. DISSOLVE TO:

147 INT. THE APARTMENT – NIGHT

Bud is in the process of packing. In the middle of the living room are several large cardboard cartons filled with his possessions. The art posters are off the walls, the bric-a-brac has been removed from the shelves, and Bud is stowing away the last of his books and records. He crosses to the fireplace, opens one of the drawers in the cabinet above it, takes out a forty-five automatic. He holds the gun in the palm of his hand, studies it appraisingly. The doorbell rings. Bud snaps out of his reverie, drops the gun into one of the cartons,

108

goes to the door and opens it. Standing outside is Dr. Dreyfuss, with a plastic ice bucket in his hand.

DR. DREYFUSS: Say, Baxter – we're having a little party and we ran out of ice – so I was wondering –

BUD: Sure, Doc.

DR. DREYFUSS (*stepping inside*): How come you're alone on New Year's Eve?

BUD: Well, I have things to do –

DR. DREYFUSS (*noticing cartons*): What's this – you packing?

BUD: Yeah – I'm giving up the apartment.

He goes into the kitchen, opens the refrigerator, starts to pry out the ice-cube trays.

DR. DREYFUSS: Where are you moving to?

BUD: I don't know. All I know is I got to get out of this place.

DR. DREYFUSS: Sorry to lose you, Baxter.

BUD: Me? Oh, you mean my body. Don't worry, Doc – it'll go to the University – I'll put it in writing –

He dumps the ice-cubes, still in their trays, into the bucket Dr. Dreyfuss is holding. Then he pulls Kirkeby's unopened bottle of champagne out of the refrigerator.

BUD: Can you use a bottle of champagne?

DR. DREYFUSS: Booze we don't need. Why don't you join us, Baxter? We got two brain surgeons, an ear, nose and throat specialist, a proctologist, and three nurses from Bellevue.

BUD: No, thanks – I don't feel like it. Look, Doc – in case I don't see you again – how much do I owe you for taking care of that girl?

DR. DREYFUSS: Forget it – I didn't do it as a doctor – I did it as a neighbor. (*stopping in doorway*) By the way, whatever happened to her?

BUD (*airily*): You know me with girls. Easy come, easy go. Goodbye, Doc.

DR. DREYFUSS: Happy New Year.

Bud closes the door, returns to the kitchen, brings out a box of glassware and the tennis racquet. As he starts to deposit the racquet in a carton, he

notices a strand of spaghetti clinging to the strings. He removes it gently, stands there twirling the limp spaghetti absently around his finger.   CUT TO:

148   INT. CHINESE RESTAURANT – NIGHT

It is five minutes before midnight, New Year's Eve. Sitting alone in the last booth is Fran, a paper hat on her head, a pensive look on her face. There are two champagne glasses on the table, and the usual noisemakers, but the chair opposite is empty. Above the general hubbub, the Chinese pianist can be heard playing. After a moment, Fran glances off.

Threading his way through the merrymakers crowding the bar and overflowing from the booths is Sheldrake. He is in dinner clothes, topped by a paper hat. Reaching the last booth, he drops into the chair facing Fran.

SHELDRAKE: Sorry it took me so long on the phone. But we're all set.

FRAN: All set for what?

SHELDRAKE: I rented a car – it's going to be here at one o'clock – we're driving to Atlantic City.

FRAN: Atlantic City?

SHELDRAKE: I know it's a drag – but you can't find a hotel room in town – not on New Year's Eve.

FRAN (*a long look at Sheldrake*): Ring out the old year, ring in the new. Ring-a-ding-ding.

SHELDRAKE: I didn't plan it this way, Fran, – actually, it's all Baxter's fault.

FRAN: Baxter?

SHELDRAKE: He wouldn't give me the key to the apartment.

FRAN: He wouldn't.

SHELDRAKE: Just walked out on me – quit – threw that big fat job right in my face.

FRAN (*a faint smile*): The nerve.

SHELDRAKE: That little punk – after all I did for him! He said I couldn't bring anybody to his apartment – especially not Miss Kubelik. What's he got against you, anyway?

FRAN (*a faraway look in her eye*): I don't know. I guess that's the way it crumbles – cookie-wise.

SHELDRAKE: What are you talking about?

FRAN: I'd spell it out for you – only I can't spell.

The piano player is consulting the watch on his upraised left arm. He drops the arm in a signal, and the lights go out. At the same time, he strikes up AULD LANG SYNE.

All over the dimly lit room, couples get to their feet, embracing and joining in the song.

In the last booth, Sheldrake leans across the table, kisses Fran.

SHELDRAKE: Happy New Year, Fran.

Fran's expression is preoccupied. Sheldrake faces in the direction of the pianist, and holding his glass aloft, sings along with others.

As AULD LANG SYNE *comes to an end, the place explodes noisily – there is a din of horns, ratchets and shouted greetings. The lights come up again. In the last booth, Sheldrake turns back toward Fran – but she is no longer there. Her paper hat lies abandoned on her vacated chair.*

SHELDRAKE: Fran – (*looking around*) – where are you, Fran?

He rises, cranes his neck, trying to spot her in the

crowd.

DISSOLVE TO:

149 EXT. BROWNSTONE HOUSE – NIGHT

Fran, a coat thrown over the dress she was wearing at the Rickshaw, comes down the street almost at a run. There is a happy, expectant look on her face. She hurries up the steps of the house and through the front door.

150 INT. STAIRCASE AND SECOND FLOOR LANDING – NIGHT

Fran mounts the stairs eagerly. As she reaches the landing and heads for Bud's apartment, there is a loud, sharp report from inside. Fran freezes momentarily, then rushes to the door.

FRAN: Mr. Baxter! (*pounding on door*) Mr. Baxter! *Mr. Baxter!*

The door opens and there stands Bud, the bottle of champagne he has just uncorked still foaming over in his hand. He stares at Fran unbelievingly.

FRAN (*sagging with relief*): Are you all right?

BUD: I'm fine.

FRAN: Are you sure? How's your knee?

BUD: I'm fine all over.

FRAN: Mind if I come in?

BUD (*still stunned*): Of course not.

151 INT. THE APARTMENT – NIGHT

Fran comes in and Bud shuts the door. The room is the same as we left it, except for an empty champagne glass standing on the coffee table.

BUD: Let me get another glass.

He goes to one of the cartons, takes out a champagne glass wrapped in newspaper, starts to unwrap it.

FRAN (*looking around*): Where are you going?

BUD: Who knows? Another neighborhood – another town – another job – I'm on my own.

FRAN: That's funny – so am I. (*Bud, pouring champagne, looks up at her*) What did you do with the cards?

BUD (*indicating carton*): In there.

Fran takes the deck of cards and the gin rummy score pad out of the carton, settles herself on the couch, starts to shuffle the cards expertly.

BUD: What about Mr. Sheldrake?

FRAN: I'm going to send him a fruit cake every Christmas.

Bud sinks down happily on the couch, and Fran holds out the deck to him.

FRAN: Cut.

Bud cuts a card, but doesn't look at it.

BUD: I love you, Miss Kubelik.

FRAN (*cutting a card*): Seven – (*looking at Bud's card*) – queen.

She hands the deck to Bud.

BUD: Did you hear what I said, Miss Kubelik? I absolutely adore you.

FRAN (*smiling*): Shut up and deal!

Bud begins to deal, never taking his eyes off her. Fran removes her coat, starts picking up her cards and arranging them. Bud, a look of pure joy on his face, deals – and deals – and keeps dealing.

And that's about it. Story-wise. FADE OUT.

The End

Photographs: Billy Wilder during the shooting of The Apartment.

THE
FORTUNE
COOKIE

Produced and directed by Billy Wilder
Written by Billy Wilder and I. A. L. Diamond
Associate Producers: I. A. L. Diamond and
 Doane Harrison
Music by André Previn
Director of Photography: Joseph La Shelle A.S.C.
Photographed in Panavision (black and white)
Art Director: Robert Luthardt
Set decoration by Edward G. Boyle
Scenic Artist: Duncan A. Spencer
Film Editor: Daniel Mandell A.C.E.
Sound: Robert Martin
Sound Editor: Wayne Fury
Music Editor: Richard Carruth
Re-recording: Buddy Myers
Production Supervisor: Allen K. Wood

Unit Manager: Patrick J. Palmer
Assistant Director: Jack N. Reddish
Properties: Frank Agnone
Script Supervisor: Marshall Walins
Special effects: Sass Bedig
Wardrobe: Chuck Arrico and Paula Giokaris
Make-up: Loren Cosand
Hairdresser: Alice Monte C.H.S.
Casting: Lynn Stalmaster
A Phalanx-Jalem Production. Copyright
 MCMLXVI by Phalanx-Jalem Productions
 and the Mirisch Corporation of Delaware
Distributed by United Artists
Length: 126 minutes
U.K. Censor Certificate: U
THE FORTUNE COOKIE
U.K. Title: *Meet Whiplash Willie*

Harry Hinkle	JACK LEMMON	The Four Specialists	BARTLETT ROBINSON
Willie Gingrich	WALTER MATTHAU		ROBERT P. LIEB
Boom Boom Jackson	RON RICH		MARTIN BLAINE
Sandy	JUDI WEST		BEN WRIGHT
Mother Hinkle	LURENE TUTTLE	Doc Schindler	NED GLASS
Charlotte Gingrich	MARGE REDMOND	Mr. Cimoli	HOWARD MCNEAR
Jeffrey Gingrich	JOHN TODD ROBERTS	Maury, the Equipment Man	HERBIE FAYE
Ginger Gingrich	LISA JILL	His Assistant	BILLY BECK
Dr. Krugman	HARRY DAVIS	Mr. Jackson	ARCHIE MOORE
Sister Veronica	ANN SHOEMAKER	Elvira	JUDY PACE
Ferret-faced Nurse	MARYESTHER DENVER	Man in Bar	BOB DOQUI
Young Intern	BILL CHRISTOPHER	Football Announcer	KEITH JACKSON
O'Brien	HARRY HOLCOMBE	TV Director	HERB ELLIS
Thompson	LES TREMAYNE	Nun	DODIE HEATH
Kincaid	LAUREN GILBERT	The Lawyers' Receptionist	HELEN KLEEB
Purkey	CLIFF OSMOND	Newscaster	DON REED
Max	NOAM PITLIK	Girl on TV	LOUISE VIENNA
Professor Winterhalter	SIG RUMAN	Tailor	JON SILO

1. The Accident

1 CLEVELAND MUNICIPAL STADIUM

It is a gloomy, bone-chilling Sunday afternoon in November. The world champion Browns are playing the Minnesota Vikings. If you haven't got a ticket, forget it. You couldn't squeeze a Honda into the parking lot, it is so clogged with cars and buses. And you couldn't shoehorn a midget into the stands, where 83,011 fans are screaming their fool heads off. So your best bet is to drive another 75 miles, till you're out of the blacked-out area, and watch the game on television.

On the field, Jim Brown dives over from the 2-yard line. The crowd is on its feet, roaring.

VOICE OVER P.A.: Jim Brown scores for Cleveland.

The teams line up for the conversion. Groza boots the ball between the uprights.

VOICE OVER P.A.: Groza's kick is good.

CAMERA PANS UP *past the cheering crowd in the stands to the TV booth on top of the stadium.*

In the booth, huddled in their overcoats, are the ANNOUNCER, his partner, two spotters, a statistician and a TV cameraman. A couple of the men are sipping coffee from cardboard containers, one is munching on a hot dog. The announcer, who has a monitor in front of him, speaks into his lavaliere mike.

ANNOUNCER: And that's the end of the first quarter – with the score Cleveland Browns 10, Minnesota Vikings 7 . . . The lights have been turned on here in Municipal Stadium – we had rain and sleet this morning – but the field was covered with tarpaulin up until game time, and the footing down there is fairly good. (*looks through his field glasses*) The teams have changed sides – and here comes the kickoff.

The ball sails off Groza's foot, is taken near the Vikings' goal-line, and run back to the 19. The crowd yells.

Outside one of the tunnels leading to the stadium stands a huge television trailer, displaying the CBS eye. A tangle of cables connects it with the field. A man comes out of the tunnel, carrying a large thermos jug of coffee, starts into the trailer. In the trailer, the TV crew is seated at a console table, casing the four monitors which are fed by the cameras on the field. The man with the thermos jug comes in, sets it down. On the monitors, a scrimmage play is in progress – we see two different angles of the same play, the crowd reacting, and the announcer in his booth.

ANNOUNCER: . . . The big Viking fullback is brought down on the 28-yard line. Bill Glass and Larry Benz were in on the tackle.

Standing away from the console, communicating by head-phone with the cameramen on the field, is the TECHNICAL DIRECTOR.

DIRECTOR: Camera Two – cover the downfield pass pattern . . . Camera Four – move down to the line of scrimmage . . .

In the stands, on the fifty-yard line, is Camera Two. The operator switches lenses.

Hurrying down the sideline is the operator of Camera Four – this is the guy we're really interested in. His name is HARRY HINKLE, and he will be 36 next September. That makes him a Virgo – and if he had read his horoscope, he would've stayed in bed today. He wears a duffel coat, knitted cap, gloves and a head-phone, and his face is blue with cold. His camera is a portable job, and he schleps it on his shoulder. A cable runs from the camera to a battery pack, which in turn is being schlepped around by his assistant. They are operating on the Browns' side of the field, and beyond them are the rolled-up tarpaulins which had covered the gridiron before the game. Reaching the line of scrimmage, Hinkle, a poet of video, takes a stance along the sideline, his eye on the finder, his lens on the ball-carrier, trying to catch an extra-nifty shot of the action.

We see this extra-nifty shot, as the Viking fullback sweeps around left end for a short gain.

In the TV booth, the announcer is looking through his field glasses.

ANNOUNCER: He only picked up half a yard. It's now fourth down, and we have a kicking situation . . . Going in as the deep men for Cleveland are 27, Walter Roberts, and 44, Luther Boom Boom Jackson.

He glances down at the monitor, BOOM BOOM JACKSON, a 220-pound Negro half-back, rises from the Cleveland bench, throws off his cape, trots out toward the field.

ANNOUNCER: So far this season, Boom Boom Jackson has averaged 28.7 yards on his punt returns – he's leading the league in that department.

In the TV trailer, the technical director is talking into his head-phone.

DIRECTOR: Camera Four – move to the thirty-yard line and cover the punt . . . Hinkle – are you there, Hinkle?

Hinkle, on the sideline, hasn't heard a word – for he has removed the head-phone, and is rubbing his frost-bitten ears. From the head-phone comes a squawking noise, and he quickly puts it back on again.

HINKLE: Yeah, this is Hinkle . . . Thirty-yard

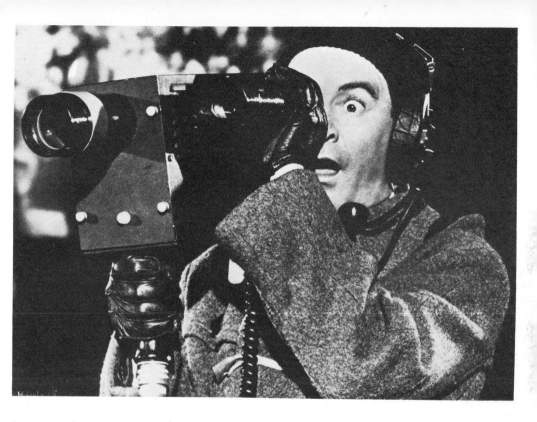

line. Roger . . . And how about some coffee for us out here – with a little anti-freeze in it ? (*to his assistant*) This way, Joe.

They move up to the yard marker and Hinkle gets set to cover the play.

The Viking kicker gets off a high, arching punt. In the Cleveland secondary, Boom Boom Jackson retreats a couple of steps, gets under the ball, gobbles it up, and instantly shifts into high gear. As he cuts toward the sideline behind his interference, twisting, dodging, straight-arming, the 83,011 people in the stands are on their feet, going wild.

Hinkle is with it all the way – panning the camera with elegant assurance, not missing one step of Boom Boom's awesome display of speed and power.

On the Viking 35, a would-be tackler sideswipes Boom Boom, breaking his stride.

Hinckle, photographing away, rears back slightly as the play comes directly toward him.

Another tackler hits Boom Boom, and he hurtles diagonally across the sideline – smack into Harry Hinckle. POW! The camera goes flying into the air, Hinckle goes flying backward. He flips over a rolled-up tarp, in a spectacular somersault, lands

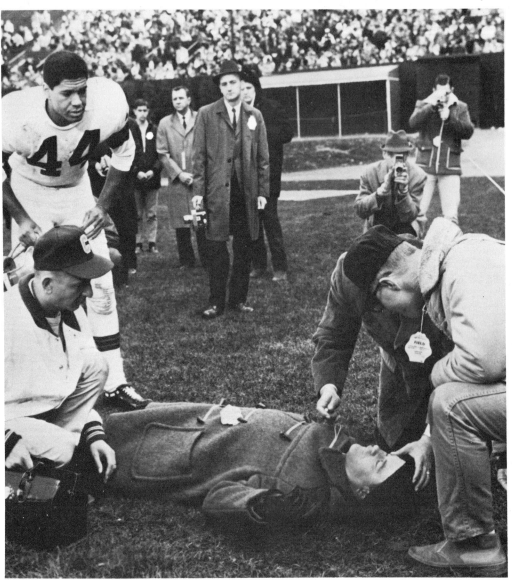

flat on his face like a sack of cement.

In the TV booth, the announcer, watching through his field glasses, is chuckling professionally.

ANNOUNCER: Looks like Boom Boom Jackson has not only racked up fifty-five yards, but also one of our cameramen.

Hinkle gets to his feet groggily. The crowd in the stands is laughing. Hinkle, a silly grin on his face, acknowledges their laughter with a wave of the hand – then his legs give out from under him, and he flops on his back, out cold.

Boom Boom Jackson vaults over the tarpaulin, kneels beside Hinkle, removing his helmet. At the same time Hinkle's assistant comes up on the other side, leans over him.

ASSISTANT (*slapping his face*): Harry!

In the stands, the crowd is still on its feet, but the gaiety has died down. A uniformed high school bandleader, looking off toward the scene of the accident, brings down his baton, and the band strikes up a march – WAVE THE FLAG. The Browns' doctor and trainer come hurrying over from the bench, examine Hinkle. Boom Boom watches worriedly as the doctor feels Hinkle's pulse, raises his eyelids, breaks an ammonia capsule and waves it under his nose. Hinkle doesn't budge. In the TV booth, the announcer, watching through his field glasses, has also sobered up.

ANNOUNCER: I hope it isn't anything serious. (*lowers glasses*) And now, while there is time out on the field, let's look at the accident again on CBS's exclusive stop-action camera.

On the monitor, we see a replay of the accident – the frame freezing as the camera flies out of Hinkle's hand, and as he tumbles backward over the tarpaulin.

ANNOUNCER (*looking through his glasses*): Oh-oh. They're bringing the ambulance on the field.

An ambulance races up along the cinder track, pulls to a stop. The driver and his aide hop out, pull a stretcher out of the back of the ambulance. A couple of policemen are now trying to hold back the still photographers gathered around the

prone figure of Hinkle. As Boom Boom looks on with concern, the two ambulance men lift Hinkle gently onto the stretcher. The referee comes up beside Boom Boom, taps him on the shoulder.

REFEREE: Come on – let's play ball.

Boom Boom reluctantly follows the referee. The driver and his aide slide the stretcher, with Hinkle on it, into the rear of the ambulance.

Boom Boom trots out on the field alongside the referee, putting his helmet on. The Browns are already in a huddle. As Boom Boom joins them, a siren starts o.s. Boom Boom glances back toward the sideline.

The ambulance, siren screaming, turret light blinking, is speeding out the gate of the stadium.

FADE OUT.

2. The Brother-in-law

2 ST. MARK'S HOSPITAL

It is a quiet Sunday evening, and business is slack. Pacing up and down the corridor, outside a pair of swinging doors marked X-RAYS, is WILLIE GINGRICH. *He is a tall, loose-jointed man of 40, with a brain full of razor blades and a heart full of chutzpah. He would have run afoul of the law a long time ago if he didn't have a slick lawyer – himself. He wears an old tweed coat and a felt hat, and is smoking nervously.*

On a bench against the wall sit MRS. HINKLE, *a wispy woman of 60, and* CHARLOTTE GINGRICH, *age 33. They are dressed for the weather outside, not for style. Charlotte may have been effervescent once, but ten years of marriage to Willie have taken all the fizz out of her. Mrs. Hinkle is crying softly into her handkerchief, and Charlotte is trying to comfort her.*

CHARLOTTE: Please, mother. He'll be all right.

MRS. HINKLE (*to Willie*): You suppose maybe it's something internal?

WILLIE: How would I know? I'm a lawyer, not a doctor.

From around a bend in the corridor whiz a couple of kids on skateboards. They are GINGER *and* JEFFREY GINGRICH, *aged 7 and 9 respectively, and they are obviously having a ball on the smooth linoleum floor.*

CHARLOTTE (*as they flash by*): Jeffrey – Ginger – cut that out! This is a hospital.

WILLIE: Let 'em. If they're going to break a leg, this is the place to do it.

The light outside the X-ray room stops blinking. As Willie pushes the double doors apart to peek in, they swing open from the inside and he rears back. A nun comes out. She is in a white habit, and her name is SISTER VERONICA.

SISTER VERONICA: I'm terribly sorry.

WILLIE: All my fault, Sister. I was trying to – (*pointing into X-ray room*) I'm his brother-in-law, Sister.

SISTER VERONICA: I see.

WILLIE (*pointing at the bench*): And this is his mother, Sister – and this is my wife – his sister – Sister.

SISTER VERONICA: How do you do.

WILLIE: We were sort of anxious to find out –

SISTER VERONICA: I understand. It'll be a few more minutes.

WILLIE: Thank you, Sister. (*as she goes off, there is another sob from Mrs. Hinkle*) Shut up, Mother.

MRS. HINKLE: Poor Harry. He was always so brittle. (*to Charlotte*) Remember when he fell off the garage?

CHARLOTTE: Oh, Mother, not that old story again.

WILLIE: What story?

MRS. HINKLE: When they were kids, in Toledo. He and Charlotte were playing paratroopers. She pushed him off the roof.

CHARLOTTE: I didn't push him – he jumped. And anyway, he had an umbrella. Is it my fault he forgot to open it?

WILLIE (*a faint gleam*): Did he hurt himself?

MRS. HINKLE. Spent two months in bed. He had a compressed vertebra.

WILLIE (*those razor blades beginning to mesh*): Compressed vertebra, huh?

Jeffrey comes whooshing up on his skateboard, makes a fancy stop.

JEFFREY: Hey, Dad – can we have a dime?

WILLIE: What for?

JEFFREY: To put in that box.

He points to a collection box hanging on the wall near the elevator. Standing beside it is Ginger.

GINGER (*calling*): It's for unwed mothers.

WILLIE: Unwed mothers? I'm for that.

He fishes some coins from his pocket, hands them to Jeffrey, who goes skating off toward the box.

The doors of the X-ray room open, and an INTERN *and a nun come out. They hold the doors back as an orderly wheels out a stretcher table. On it lies Harry Hinkle, in a hospital gown and covered to his chin with a sheet.*

Mrs. Hinkle and Charlotte jump to their feet, converge on Harry.

MRS. HINKLE: Harry – Harry baby – how do you feel?

A groggy Harry half-opens his eyes and tries to focus.

MRS. HINKLE: It's me – Mama – and Charlotte is here and Willie and Ginger and Jeffrey –

HARRY (*a wan smile*): Hi, sports fans.

WILLIE (*to the intern*): How is he, Doc?

INTERN: He has a mild concussion. We've put him under sedation – he'll rest comfortably tonight.

HARRY (*mumbling*): This is Harry Hinkle on Camera Four –

MRS. HINKLE (*a sob*): He doesn't even know his own mother.

WILLIE: Any broken bones? Ruptures? Internal bleeding?

INTERN: I don't think so.

WILLIE: You don't think so! How long have you been out of medical school?

INTERN: Five months.

WILLIE: That long, huh?

INTERN (drawing himself up): Sir?

HARRY (mumbling): Okay, Louie. You pick up the band, I'll pan with the pom-pom girls. (feebly starts humming 'Wave the Flag')

INTERN (pretty angry by now; to orderly): Let's go.

The orderly starts wheeling Harry off.

WILLIE: Wait a minute! Where are you taking him?

INTERN: To the general ward.

WILLIE: Oh no you don't. I want a private room for him – and nurses around the clock – nothing is too good for my brother-in-law.

INTERN (to nun): You'd better check with the admission office.

WILLIE: And don't let's have any of that red tape, Sister. (to orderly) Take him upstairs.

INTERN (sarcastically): How about the penthouse suite?

WILLIE: Now you're talking.

The orderly wheels Harry toward the elevator, followed by the intern and the nun.

MRS. HINKLE (sobbing): They're not going to cut him open, are they?

WILLIE: Shut up, Mother. Charlotte, take her home – take everybody home.

CHARLOTTE: Aren't you coming?

WILLIE: No.

CHARLOTTE: What about dinner?

WILLIE: To hell with it. I'm not letting him out of my sight – not for a minute. (moves toward elevator)

CHARLOTTE (beckoning to the kids): Ginger – Jeffrey – we're on our way.

JEFFREY (pouting): Aw, we want to skate some more.

CHARLOTTE: You can play at home.

WILLIE (over his shoulder): Yeah. Why don't you teach them that paratrooper game?

Willie watches as Harry is loaded into the elevator, and the doors close. He stands there for a beat, pensive. Then he heads toward a telephone booth. As he reaches into his pocket for a dime, he realizes he has given away all his change. He is stymied, but being Willie Gingrich, it takes him only a second to come up with a solution. He crosses to the collection can – the one for unwed mothers – takes it off the wall, and hiding it with his body, shakes it until a coin falls out. He hangs the can back in place, returns to the phone booth, steps inside. He drops the dime into the slot, dials a number.

WILLIE (into phone): Cleveland Plain-Dealer? Give me the City Desk . . . Hello? This is William H. Gingrich, attorney-at-law. I represent Harry Hinkle – the cameraman who was hurt at the game today? This may be of some interest to you – I'm suing CBS, the Cleveland Browns, and the Municipal Stadium for one million dollars . . . That's right, a million dollars . . . Hinkle, H-I-N-K-L-E. . . . St. Mark's Hospital. . . . he's very serious . . . and so am I!   FADE

3. The Caper

3 EXT. ST. MARK'S HOSPITAL

It is a gray, cold Monday morning. A late-model white Cadillac Coupe de Ville pulls into a parking place in front of the hospital, and out steps Boom Boom Jackson. He is a sharp dresser off the field – wears a dark business suit, tab-collar shirt, narrow tie, camel's hair coat with the collar turned up, no hat. He carries a bouquet of flowers which must have set him back twenty dollars. He hurries up the steps, enters the building.

4 FOURTH FLOOR – HOSPITAL

Behind the reception desk, a nun is sorting index cards. The elevator doors open, and Boom Boom comes out, the flowers in his hand. He crosses to the desk.

BOOM BOOM: Mr. Hinkle's room – what's the

number?

NUN (*working away*): Sorry, but it's not visiting hours.

BOOM BOOM: I thought maybe you could make an exception – you see, I'm the guy that –

NUN (*glances up, recognizes him*): Oh. (*confidentially*) Can I ask you something, Mr. Jackson?

BOOM BOOM: Sure.

NUN: What do you think our chances are against the Philadelphia Eagles? Because Sister Veronica wants thirteen points.

BOOM BOOM: You bet around here?

NUN: Certainly. I already owe her a coke from last week.

BOOM BOOM: Well, I can't say anything – it's against League regulations – I could be suspended –

NUN: I understand. (*pointing*) He's in 403 – right down the corridor.

BOOM BOOM: Thank you. (*starts down the corridor; over his shoulder, in a whisper*) Give her twelve-and-a-half points.

She smiles after him.

5 INT. HOSPITAL ROOM

It's no penthouse suite, but it's single-occupancy, with a bathroom, and a small television set mounted high on the wall opposite the bed. Early morning light filters in through the lowered shade. Harry Hinkle is asleep in bed. In a chair, working on a crossword puzzle, by the light of a table lamp, is a middle-aged, ferret-faced, civilian NURSE. Snoozing in an armchair is Willie. His collar is open and his tie loosened, and he is using his tweed coat as a blanket.

There is a tentaitve knock on the door. The nurse gets out of the chair, crosses to the door, opens it. Boom Boom is standing outside.

NURSE: Yes?

BOOM BOOM: This *is* Mr. Hinkle's room.

NURSE: That's right.

BOOM BOOM: How is he? I called a couple of times last night, but they wouldn't give me any information.

Willie's eyes are open now and he is watching them.

NURSE: I wouldn't know about his condition. He's still asleep.

BOOM BOOM: Oh. (*a beat*) I guess I better wait outside.

NURSE: You do that.

As she closes the door on Boom Boom, Willie gets out of his chair, stretching.

WILLIE: How about that guy? He's got some nerve showing up here. (*he runs his hand over his unshaven chin*) You wouldn't have a razor on you, would you? (*a dirty look from the nurse*) Whatever happened to all those beautiful nurses you see on television?

He has crossed to the window and pulled the shade. It flies up with a sharp snap.

The sound reaches Harry. He stirs, mumbles. Willie looks at him, then turns to the nurse.

WILLIE: Would you mind leaving us alone for a while?

NURSE (*acidly*): I'd be delighted.

She stalks out the door. Harry blinks his eyes open, looks around the room, trying to get his bearings.

WILLIE: Good morning, Harry.

HARRY: How did I get here?

WILLIE: By stretcher and ambulance.

HARRY (*trying to sit up*) Oooh, my head. What did they give me?

WILLIE: A whole gang of sleeping pills.

HARRY (*pulling the bed-covers aside*): Where's

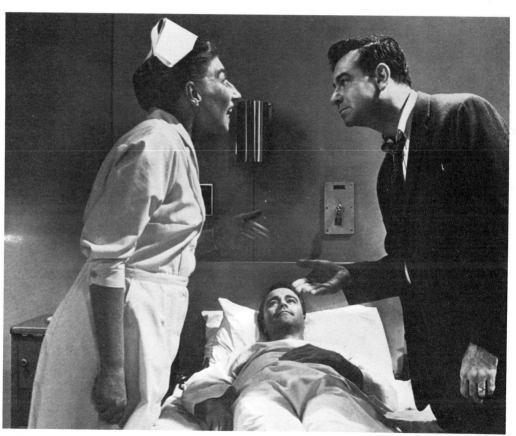

the can?

WILLIE: Forget it. You can't get out of bed.

HARRY: Who says?

WILLIE (*lighting a cigarette*): I hate to break it to you, kid – but you got a spinal injury.

HARRY: *What?*

WILLIE: Your left leg is numb, and you got no feeling in the first three fingers of your right hand.

Harry looks at his hand in panic, then slowly starts wiggling his fingers.

HARRY: You're crazy. I can move my hand – (*flexes his left leg under the covers*) *And* my leg.

WILLIE: Sure you can – if you want to blow a million bucks.

HARRY: A million – ? What are you talking about?

WILLIE: That's what we're suing for. They'll offer a hundred thousand, and we'll settle for a quarter of a million.

HARRY (*a beat*): I got to go to the can.

WILLIE (*pushing him back*): Stay where you are. I'll bring it to you.

He goes into the bathroom. Harry sits up again.

HARRY: What are you trying to pull? I'm perfectly all right.

WILLIE (*from bathroom*): If there's one thing I hate it's a patient who makes his own diagnosis. (*comes out carrying a bedpan*)

HARRY: This is ridiculous. There's nothing wrong with me.

WILLIE: That's what you think. Not only can't you move your hand and your leg, but you had this concussion – so now you got this ringing in your ears and double vision.

HARRY: Double vision?

WILLIE: How many of me do you see?

HARRY: *One.* One cheap, chiseling shyster lawyer who, of all people, had to marry my sister.

WILLIE: Nice talk. I'm handing you a quarter of a million dollars, on a silver platter – (*he holds out the bedpan*)

128

HARRY: I don't want the money – and I don't want the silver platter.

He shoves the bedpan aside, bounces out of bed, and heads for the can.

WILLIE (*following him*): What's the matter – you feel sorry for insurance companies?

Harry disappears into the bathroom, slamming the door in Willie's face. Willie continues to talk through the closed door.

WILLIE: They've got so much money they don't know what to do with it – they've run out of storage space – they have to microfilm it. What's a quarter of a million to them? They take it out of petty cash. So don't give me with the scruples.

There is a knock on the door. Willie looks around apprehensively, then half-opens the door. It's Boom Boom.

WILLIE (*sharply*): What is it?

BOOM BOOM: The nurse said he was awake.

WILLIE: Look, pal, can't you read? (*points to NO VISITORS sign*) We got a sick man here.

BOOM BOOM: How sick is he? Nobody will tell me anything.

WILLIE: Why don't you just leave the flowers? I'll give them to him.

BOOM BOOM: (*stepping back*) No, thanks. Maybe I can see him later.

Willie closes the door – just in time – because Harry is coming out of the bathroom. He is clutching the split back of the hospital gown.

HARRY: They put you in these things just to humiliate you.

Willie shushes him, points to the door.

HARRY (*looking around*): All right – where are my clothes?

WILLIE: Why?

HARRY: I'm checking out of this place.

WILLIE: Checking out? Where do you think you are, in a Hilton Hotel? You're not registered here – you're *booked* here. You got a number on your wrist. (*indicates identification bandage*).

HARRY: Well, what do I need – a reprieve from

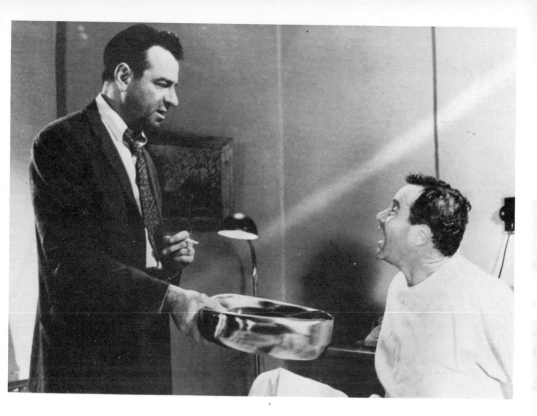

the Governor?

WILLIE: No, a discharge from the doctor. Now get back in bed.

HARRY: Okay. But only because it's draughty – and I got no pants.

He climbs into bed, pulls the covers up. Willie circles the bed, eyeing Harry like a prosecutor about to work over an unfriendly witness.

WILLIE (*the gentle overture*): Harry, puppy, how much do you make a week? I mean, how much are you left with after withholding, and supporting your mother, and paying alimony –

HARRY: All right, so I owe you sixty dollars.

WILLIE (*stabs cigarette out in the bedpan*): It's not that, Harry. It's just that I don't want my brother-in-law to be a nobody. I want to see you in a fastback Mustang, Italian silk suits, a decent apartment – a go go, baby – all the way.

HARRY: Willie, I'm not going to stand still for one of your phony whiplash cases.

WILLIE: Whiplash, nothing. We're going for all the marbles.

HARRY: I wouldn't even lift a finger to –

WILLIE (*building*): That's all you have to do – *not* lift a finger. Think of your mother –

bronchitis every winter – she shouldn't be in Cleveland – she should be in Florida – baking her chest. And your sister – 33 years old, never had a fur coat. Then there's your nephew and your niece – they have to sleep in the same room – you want them to wind up going to an analyst?

HARRY: You want me to wind up going to jail?

WILLIE: That's negative thinking. Sure those insurance guys are tough and they're smart. But I'm just as tough – and I know all their tricks. They'll hit you with hammers, they'll stick pins into you –

HARRY: Not me.

WILLIE: All you have to remember is which nerves are damaged. (*takes Harry's right hand*) From the middle of your ring finger to your thumb – you're numb. As for your leg –

HARRY: Don't lose yourself in details.

WILLIE: I don't care if they get a hundred doctors to examine you – if you say your back is killing you, they can't prove it isn't. That's what we call pain and suffering – and the money you get for that is tax-free.

HARRY: What pain? What suffering?

WILLIE: You never can tell about back injuries. You may think you're all right – but six months from now, you suddenly start having dizzy spells, muscle spasms, sciatica – you can't work any more. *Then* try to collect.

HARRY: There's nothing wrong with my back – if you'd just get off it.

The door opens and the ferret-faced nurse comes in with a tray. On it are a pot of coffee, dry toast, and a dish of stewed prunes.

NURSE: Breakfast!

She hands the tray to Willie, starts to crank up the bed.

NURSE (*to Harry*): I thought you'd like some nice stewed prunes. We must keep regular.

HARRY (*cranked up to a sitting position*): Where's that damn doctor?

NURSE (*reproving*): Dr. Krugman is making his

rounds. He'll be here shortly with your X-rays.

WILLIE: Thank you, nurse. (*as she starts out, he indicates Harry*): And bring *him* some breakfast, too.

She shoots him a look, exits. Willie settles himself in the chair, with the tray on his lap, starts eating.

HARRY: Did you hear that? X-rays. There goes your whole cockamamie case.

WILLIE: Oh, yeah? What about your little mishap when you were with the paratroopers?

HARRY: What paratroopers?

WILLIE: You and Charlotte – on the garage roof – in Toledo? (*pantomimes downward plunge*) You had that compressed vertebra, remember?

HARRY: That was like thirty years ago.

WILLIE: That's the beauty of it. The doctor who treated you is long gone. And with a vertebra, you can't tell an old injury from a new one. So who'll ever know?

HARRY: *I* will. Look, Willie, I'm not saying I'm any better than the next guy – maybe I add a few bucks to my expense account – but an out-and-out fake like this –

WILLIE: Fake? We got 83,000 eyewitnesses – another thirty million watched it on television. They saw you get hit by that 220-pound monster – they saw you take a spill over that tarpaulin, which shouldn't have been there in the first place. So we have a clear-cut case of negligence. (*sips his coffee*) If you think that gown is humiliating, wait till you taste this coffee.

HARRY: Where do you think you are, in a Hilton Hotel?

WILLIE: The way I see it, their lawyers won't even let it come to trial – they know how juries love to soak an insurance company. And when I wheel you into that courtroom –

HARRY: *Wheel* me in?

WILLIE: Sure. You're going to be in a chair – and wear one of those corsets –

HARRY: Wanna bet?

WILLIE: It's only until we collect the money. Then you make a gradual recovery –

The phone rings.

HARRY: I'm going to make a rapid recovery. Starting right now.

As Willie crosses to the phone, Harry gets out of bed, rips off the identification bandage, tries to untie his gown.

WILLIE (*into phone*): I told you, no calls . . . New York? Okay, I'll take it . . . Hello? Yes, this is Harry Hinkle's room. Who wants him? . . . WHO? . . . You don't say! (*holds phone out to Harry*) The next voice you hear will be your wife.

HARRY (*flatly*): I have no wife.

WILLIE: All right, so it's your ex-wife.

HARRY: Tell her to drop dead.

WILLIE (*into phone*): I'm sorry, Sandy, but he can't talk right now.

HARRY: Or any other time. Hang up!

WILLIE (*to Harry*): Sssh! (*into phone*) Yes, Sandy, it's true. Did you see it on television?

6   INT. NEW YORK APARTMENT

It's in the West Sixties – one room, bath, kitchenette – rents for ninety dollars a month. The place is cramped and untidy – clothes all over the place, dirty dishes, a bass drum with the initials G. G. A man is asleep in a rumpled Murphy bed, his back to CAMERA.

Sitting at the kitchen table, in f.g., is SANDY HINKLE. *She is 28, blonde, wears a shortie night-gown. Even with her hair in disarray, and without makeup, there is something very provocative about her – not too much class, but instant sex.*

On the table are an open copy of the New York Daily News, a cup of coffee, and the phone on an extension cord. She speaks in an undertone, glancing back occasionally toward the sleeping figure in b.g.

SANDY (*into phone*): No, it's in the paper this morning – but all it says is they carried him off

unconscious and you're suing . . . How bad is he?

7   INT. HOSPITAL ROOM

Willie on the phone, Harry listening grimly.

WILLIE (*into phone*): Well, we don't know yet – but it's going to take more than a Band-Aid, I can tell you that.

Harry slides across the bed, grabs the phone away from him.

HARRY: Listen, you bitch, if it's the alimony you're worried about . . . Come off it, Sandy, why else would you be calling me?

8   INT. NEW YORK APARTMENT

SANDY (*into phone*): You don't have to believe me, Harry – but isn't it possible that I'm worried about *you* – that I just wanted to find out how you felt?

9   INT. HOSPITAL ROOM

As Harry vents his wrath into the phone, Willie is studying him.

HARRY (*into phone*): Isn't that touching? You didn't care how I felt a year ago – when you ran off with Gus Gilroy – didn't even leave a note – just a stale meatloaf in the refrigerator. For a whole month there I was going nuts – trying to find the laundry where you'd taken my shirts.

10   INT. NEW YORK APARTMENT

SANDY (*into phone*): Please, Harry – this is no time to . . . (*the man in bed turns over, but doesn't wake*) Well, it was your fault, too – because you're too nice a person, and too kind – you should have run after me and belted me a few and dragged me back.

11   INT. HOSPITAL ROOM

HARRY (*into phone; sizzling*): You're lucky I didn't – because I would've strangled you with one of Gus Gilroy's fancy ties – that's how nice and kind I am!

The time has come for Willie to step in. He snatches the phone from Harry's hand.

WILLIE (*into phone*): Don't mind him, Sandy – he had a concussion – he doesn't know what he's saying. . . . Well, it may be a couple of days before we have the doctor's reports – where can I reach you? . . . Don't worry, baby, if your friend answers, I'll hang up . . . Okay, if it's more convenient, you call here. Bye, Sandy.

He puts the phone down.

HARRY (*angrily*): Of all the miserable broads. I don't know what I saw in her in the first place. Cooks like a pig, smokes in bed – (*holding his hands out in front of him, palms down*) – used to walk around like a zombie, because her nail-polish was always wet – that's unless she was crawling around on her knees, trying to find one of her contact lenses. Best thing that ever happened to me was when she cut out.

WILLIE (*quietly*): Still crazy about her, huh?

HARRY: And stupid? Never read a book in her life – well, she read one book – THE CARPET-BAGGERS – and after six months, she was on page nineteen. We had no life together – no dialogue – no laughs –

WILLIE: You know, Harry, I've seen guys carry a torch before – but you're the champ. You could carry it from Greece to Mexico City, to open the next Olympic Games.

HARRY: *Me?*

WILLIE: You.

HARRY: You're out of your skull. You know how many girls I've had since Sandy? (*counting on the fingers of his right hand*) There was Phyllis – and Sheila – and Janet –

WILLIE: Use the other hand! That one's numb.

HARRY: So don't give me with that torch. Because as far as I'm concerned –

WILLIE: And the funny thing is – she still cares about you.

HARRY: The hell she does.

WILLIE: Did you hear her on the phone?

She was practically crying. And the next time she calls, and hears what shape you're in – mangled and helpless – she's going to hop the first plane from New York. You play along with me, and you'll get your wife back.

HARRY: Who wants her?

WILLIE: You do. Because you still love her.

Harry just stares at Willie, stuck for an answer. There is the sound of the door opening. Willie looks off.

Into the room comes DR. KRUGMAN, *a stocky, middle-aged man, gray-haired and short-tempered. The pockets of his white jacket are bulging with the tools of his trade. With him is Sister Veronica, carrying a batch of X-rays in their brown envelopes.*

DR. KRUGMAN (*to Sister Veronica*): So we open the kid up, and what do you think we find? Three buttons, a thumb tack, and twenty-seven cents in change.

WILLIE: Good morning, doctor.

DR. KRUGMAN: 'Morning. (*to Sister Veronica*) The parents couldn't afford to pay for the operation, so I kept the twenty-seven cents.

He turns to Harry, who is sitting up in bed, staring straight ahead.

DR. KRUGMAN: I'm Dr. Krugman. How're you feeling today?

Willie watching Harry with controlled anxiety.

HARRY: Pretty good.

WILLIE: He means – considering. What do the X-rays show?

DR. KRUGMAN: I'm kind of curious myself. I was sitting on the forty-yard line. (*rolling his eyes up*) Oy, gevalt!

He takes the X-ray from Sister Veronica, steps to the window, holds it up against the light to study it.

DR. KRUGMAN: H'mmmm.

WILLIE (*peering over his shoulder*): You said it, doctor.

HARRY: Sister, would you mind cranking the bed down?

SISTER VERONICA: Yes, indeed.

She starts to turn the crank. The head of the mattress and Harry descend together. But suddenly it is just the mattress that is moving – Harry is frozen in mid-air at a curious angle.

HARRY (*a cry of pain*): Ooooh.

WILLIE: What's the matter?

HARRY (*groaning*): My back! Crank it up, crank it up!

Sister Veronica rapidly cranks the mattress up, till it meets Harry's back.

WILLIE (*concern in his voice, but a gleam in his eye*): Does it hurt much?

DR. KRUGMAN (*still studying X-ray*): I should hope so. He's got a compressed vertebra.

WILLIE: Oh?

HARRY: I got what?

DR. KRUGMAN (*showing him the X-ray*): Look at this – there's a compression of the fifth vertebra, and a narrowed disc –

WILLIE: Are you sure?

DR. KRUGMAN (*indicating white coat*): Why do you think I'm wearing this outfit – because I'm a barber?

WILLIE: Oh, I didn't mean to question your competence.

DR. KRUGMAN: So don't kibitz. (*to Harry*) Now just relax. (*cups his hand under Harry's chin*) Tell me if this hurts. (*twist Harry's head to left, then right, and back*)

HARRY: Ooo – ow – oh –

WILLIE: Poor kid!

Harry's moans of pain bring Boom Boom in from the corridor. He stands in the open doorway, flowers in hand, peering off anxiously. Dr. Krugman is still manipulating Harry's chin, and Harry keeps moaning.

WILLIE (*lighting a cigarette*): Take it easy, Doc.

DR. KRUGMAN: I said no kibitzing.

He takes a blood-pressure apparatus out of his pocket, buttons the tourniquet around Harry's left arm.

HARRY (*to Willie, weakly*): Can I have that cigarette?

WILLIE (*to Dr. Krugman*): All right if he smokes?

DR. KRUGMAN: Personally, I gave it up. (*to Harry*) But if you got to smoke, blow a little of it my way.

He pumps up the blood-pressure apparatus. Willie passes the cigarette to Harry, who holds it stiffly between the little finger and ring finger of his right hand. Dr. Krugman has read the blood pressure, and as he removes the tourniquet, he notices the awkward way Harry is smoking.

DR. KRUGMAN: Why are you holding the cigarette like that?

HARRY: Because the other fingers are sort of numb.

WILLIE: Did you say numb?

DR. KRUGMAN: You heard him.

WILLIE: I don't understand, Doc – if he hurt his back – what's that got to do with the fingers?

DR. KRUGMAN: It's quite normal in a case like this. The vertebra must be pressing on the nerve ending – it all connects up.

WILLIE: That a fact?

DR. KRUGMAN: It's like a watch that's been run over by a locomotive.

Boom Boom takes a couple of tentative steps into the room, listening intently to the diagnosis.

DR. KRUGMAN: Imagine what happens to the springs, and the wheels, and the balance.

HARRY (*feebly*): I guess I'm lucky I'm still ticking.

Dr. Krugman takes the cigarette away from him, puffs on it once, hands it to Willie. Then he pulls a pin from his lapel, picks up Harry's right hand.

DR. KRUGMAN: Now tell me when this feels sharp – and when it feels dull.

He starts pricking Harry's hand in various spots with the pin.

HARRY: Dull – dull – sharp – dull – sharp – sharp –

Willie is mouthing the words along with Harry – like a parent sweating it out at a child's recitation.

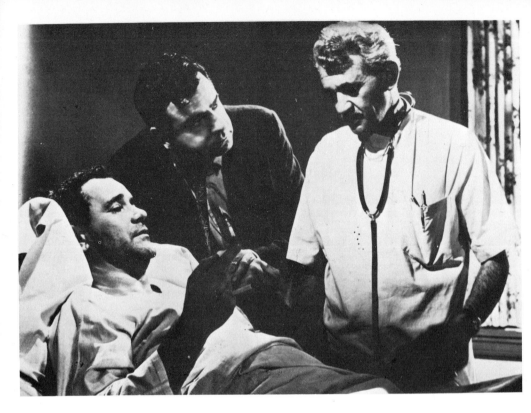

Boom Boom, involved in Harry's plight, is drawn to the bed.

BOOM BOOM (*to Harry, gently*): We got this trainer on the team – Doc Murphy – he's just great with this kind of stuff. Because us players, we get clobbered all the time –

WILLIE (*to Boom Boom*): Outside!

BOOM BOOM: – he'll just give you a massage, and put you in a whirlpool –

WILLIE (*the thumb*): I said out!

Harry glares at him, turns to Boom Boom.

HARRY: You're Boom Boom Jackson.

BOOM BOOM: Yeah. I brought you these.

He holds out the flowers to Harry. Willie intercepts them.

WILLIE: Thanks. (*hands flowers to Sister Veronica*) Sister, would you please put these in a vase? (*to Boom Boom*) 'Bye now. Very thoughtful of you.

Sister Veronica exits with the flowers. Boom Boom starts forlornly to the door.

HARRY: How did the game come out?

BOOM BOOM (*stopping*): They kicked a field goal in the last five seconds.

HARRY: Oh?

BOOM BOOM: Because I fumbled on the twelve-yard line.

HARRY (*sympathetic*): That's tough.

The ferret-faced nurse comes in with another breakfast tray.

NURSE (*smugly*): They're charging you for a second breakfast.

She puts the tray down on the bureau. Dr. Krugman has taken a metal hammer out of his pocket, and is hitting Harry's right forearm, to test his reflexes.

DR. KRUGMAN: Ever had a previous back injury?

HARRY: Huh?

DR. KRUGMAN: Maybe when you were a child?

HARRY (*stalling*): Now let me see – (*an evasive action*) The phone! Why doesn't one of you nurses answer the phone?

WILLIE: What phone?

HARRY: It's ringing.

Willie looks at Dr. Krugman with apparent concern – there is no phone ringing.

DR. KRUGMAN (*to Harry*): How many nurses do you see?

HARRY (*looking directly at nurse*): Two.

WILLIE: *Two?*

HARRY: Can we afford them?

WILLIE (*to Dr. Krugman*): Don't tell me *this* is normal.

DR. KRUGMAN: Somebody pull that shade down.

BOOM BOOM: I'll do it.

He hurries to the window, lowers the shade. The room is in semi-darkness. Dr. Krugman takes a pencil flashlight out of his pocket.

DR. KRUGMAN (*to Harry*): Open your eyes wide. Look at him.

Him is Boom Boom. Harry opens his eyes wide, focuses on Boom Boom. Dr. Krugman shines the light into his pupils. Boom Boom looks at Harry with compassion. Harry turns his eyes away.

DR. KRUGMAN: No – look where I told you. (*Harry focuses on Boom Boom again*) H'mmmm.

Nice retina.

HARRY: Thank you.

Dr. Krugman snaps the flashlight off, raises the window shade.

WILLIE: What is it, Doc? Any brain damage? Give it to us straight. We can take it.

DR. KRUGMAN: Just a simple concussion. All he needs is a little bed rest.

WILLIE: Thank God. (*a second thought*) But actually, it's the back that's bothering me.

DR. KRUGMAN: Bothering *you*?

WILLIE: I mean, with those nerves all connected up – if it affects his hand – (*looking at Harry*) – how do we know it doesn't affect some other part of his body?

HARRY (*he can take a hint*): If you don't mind, I'm going to have my breakfast. (*he throws the covers back*)

DR. KRUGMAN: Don't you move!

It's too late. Harry is out of bed, takes a couple of steps toward the breakfast tray. As he puts his weight on his left leg, it buckles under him. He staggers and almost sprawls on the floor, but at the last second Boom Boom catches him.

HARRY (*a heart-rending whimper*): My leg. I got no feeling in my left leg.

Boom Boom, cradling Harry in his arms, looks up helplessly at Dr. Krugman.

DR. KRUGMAN: Put him back in bed. Careful now.

Boom Boom carries Harry over to the bed, puts him down gently.

WILLIE: Look, Doc, I don't want to kibitz – but I don't like the looks of this – not at all.

Ignoring him, Dr. Krugman picks up the X-ray, re-examines it.

BOOM BOOM (*pulling the covers over Harry*): I'm sorry, buddy – I didn't mean to hurt you – honest I didn't – I never hurt anybody in my life – not even when they played dirty.

HARRY (*ill at ease*): You couldn't help it – it was just one of those things.

BOOM BOOM: You're gonna get well, aren't you,

135

buddy – you gotta – you just gotta – for me.
Harry smiles wanly, nods.
At the window, Willie is studying the X-ray over Dr. Krugman's shoulder.
WILLIE: If you want a layman's opinion –
DR. KRUGMAN: I do not. Nurse! (*the ferret-faced nurse comes up*) There must be a lower back injury as well. Get ahold of Dr. Montgomery. I'll want some more X-rays – and let's get ready for an encephalogram, an EMG, and if necessary, a spinal tap.
During this, Sister Veronica has returned with Boom Boom's flowers in a vase.
NURSE: Yes, Doctor. (*she exits*)
SISTER VERONICA: Anything *I* can do?
WILLIE (*a long look at Harry*): Pray for him, Sister.   FADE.

4. The Legal Eagles

12   EXT. TERMINAL BUILDING – DAY
The landmark in downtown Cleveland. Everybody who is anybody has his office there – and a few nobodies.

13   ANTEROOM – LAW OFFICE
Judging from the size and the décor, this is a thriving outfit. Behind a railing, a dozen secretaries and stenographers are hard at work. In f.g., a RECEPTIONIST *is busy at a switchboard.*
RECEPTIONIST (*into phone*): O'Brien, Thompson and Kincaid, good afternoon. . . . Sorry, Mr. O'Brien is in conference – with Mr. Thompson, and Mr. Kincaid. . . . Oh, just a minute. (*she works the plugs*) Mr. O'Brien? I know you're not to be disturbed – but it's Consolidated Insurance – the office of the vice-president.

14   INT. O'BRIEN'S OFFICE
It is very prosperous, very sedate – all mahogany
136

panelling and leather upholstery. A fire is burning in the fireplace, and the walls are lined with shelves of law books, diplomas, portraits of Supreme Court justices.
Sitting behind a massive desk, phone in hand, is O'BRIEN – *he is the senior partner. Also present are his associates –* THOMPSON *and* KINCAID, *puffing away on fat cigars. In the chair facing the desk is a heavy-set man in a shabby overcoat. His name is* PURKEY, *and he has a cheap briefcase open on his lap.*
O'BRIEN (*into phone*): All right, put him through . . . Yes, Mr. Dalrymple . . . Of course we know it's a million dollars . . . Of course we know it isn't chicken feed . . . Please, Mr. Dalrymple, you've got three grown-up lawyers handling this case. We have the hospital report right here – and we've got the Purkey Investigating Agency working on it. So you just sit back and leave the worrying to us. (*hangs up*) Go on, Mr. Purkey.
PURKEY (*consulting his notes*): In 1959, Harry Hinkle collected eighteen dollars for a raincoat he'd lost in a movie theatre. The coat was ultimately recovered, and he returned the eighteen dollars. Otherwise, there is no record that Mr. Hinkle has ever filed a claim against any insurance company in the United States.
O'BRIEN: I guess the young man is clean. Now let's see – who's his attorney?
THOMPSON: William Gingrich.
O'BRIEN (*trying to place the name*): Gingrich – Gingrich –
THOMPSON: You know – Whiplash Willie.
O'BRIEN: Oh, *him* again. (*getting up from behind the desk*) Well, gentlemen, I guess our first step is to have Hinkle examined by our own team of doctors.
KINCAID: For that, of course, we need the consent of the plaintiff.
O'BRIEN: Get Gingrich on the phone.
THOMPSON: He's not only Hinkle's lawyer – he's his brother-in-law.

KINCAID (*picking up phone*): Honey, get me William Gingrich – I think his office is somewhere in this building.

15   INT. GINGRICH OFFICE

Judging from the size and décor, this is not a thriving outfit. Just a hole in the wall, a beaten-up roll-top desk piled with unfiled papers, an old typewriter, a hot-plate with a coffee pot on it, a wall-calendar advertizing a bail bondsman.

Willie is sitting at the desk, lighting a cigarette. In a chair facing him is MR. CIMOLI, *an elderly man in an overcoat, holding a pair of crutches in his hand.*

WILLIE: Now tell me, Mr. Cimoli – exactly how did you break your hip?

CIMOLI: It's my pelvis.

WILLIE: All right, your pelvis. How did it happen?

CIMOLI: I was coming out of this store – and there it was on the sidewalk.

WILLIE: What?

Cimoli has taken a paper bag out of his pocket, and from it he produces a brown, withered banana peel.

CIMOLI: This.

WILLIE: I see. You were coming out of *what* store?

CIMOLI: Nat's Delicatessen, on Euclid Avenue.

WILLIE: Too bad.

CIMOLI: Such pain.

WILLIE: I mean, too bad it didn't happen further down the street – in front of the May Company. From *them* you can collect! Couldn't you have dragged yourself another twenty feet?

The phone is ringing by now. Willie picks it up.

WILLIE (*into phone*): Hello? . . . Speaking . . . O'Brien, Thompson and Kincaid? What can I do for you? . . . The Hinkle case? Oh, yeah, I'm handling that . . . Well, I can't talk now – I have an office full of people – suppose I come up to your place?

He hangs up, rises, gathers some typewritten pages from the desk, folds them, slips them into the inside pocket of his coat.

CIMOLI: How much do you think my pelvis is worth?

WILLIE: By itself, nothing. So it's a good thing you came to me. Before we're through with them, we'll have them begging for mercy.

CIMOLI: Who's them?

WILLIE: *That* I haven't figured out yet. But don't go away. I'll think of an angle.

He exits.

16   INT. O'BRIEN'S OFFICE

The three partners and Mr. Purkey in conference.

THOMPSON: This guy is so full of angles, and gimmicks, and twists . . . he starts to describe a doughnut, and it comes out a pretzel.

O'BRIEN: Nevertheless, when he gets here, I suggest we try the friendly approach.

THOMPSON: Okay. But after you shake hands with him, I suggest you count your fingers.

PURKEY (*rising*): I better get out of here. (*puts on hat and muffler*)

O'BRIEN: Purkey, I want you to keep digging away.

PURKEY: My pleasure. I'd like to dig a nice deep hole for our friend Gingrich.

He exits.

17   ANTEROOM – LAW OFFICE

Purkey comes out of the inner office, taking a pair of gloves out of his pocket. The hall door opens, and Willie comes in.

WILLIE: Hi there, Purkey old boy. (*he grabs his hand, pumps it*)

PURKEY: Hello.

WILLIE: They keeping you busy?

PURKEY: I'm not complaining.

He crosses to the hall door, putting on his gloves, while Willie steps up to the receptionist.

WILLIE: I'm to see O'Brien, Thompson and Kincaid.

RECEPTIONIST: And you are – ?

WILLIE: Gingrich, Gingrich and Gingrich.
Purkey, half-way out the door, looks down at his right hand, sees that the middle-finger of his glove is dangling empty.
PURKEY (*panicking*): Hey!
WILLIE (*turning*): What's the matter?
Purkey discovers that his middle finger is not missing – it just didn't wind up in the right slot. He quickly slips the finger into the glove.
PURKEY (*embarrassed*): Nothing.
He exits.
RECEPTIONIST (*to Willie*): Go right in, Mr. Gingrich.

WILLIE: Thanks. And take the rest of the afternoon off.
He starts into the inner office.

18   INT. O'BRIEN'S OFFICE
The three partners assume a friendly air as Willie enters jauntily.
WILLIE: Gentlemen –
He extends his hand to O'Brien, who deftly avoids it.
O'BRIEN: Ah, Mr. Gingrich. I've heard a lot about you. Sit down.
WILLIE (*casing the layout*): Say! You each have

138

an office like this, or do you all bunk together?

O'BRIEN: The reason we called you up here, Mr. Gingrich, is because –

WILLIE (*lowering himself into chair*): Let me guess. You want to settle.

O'BRIEN: Settle?

WILLIE (*freezing in mid-air*) You *don't* want to settle.

O'BRIEN: Certainly not.

WILLIE: That settles *that.* (*rises as if to go*)

THOMPSON: You've got no case, Gingrich. It's a simple matter of workmen's compensation.

WILLIE: It's a simple matter of *negligence.* That tarpaulin should have been rolled back fifty feet – and it's going to cost you twenty thousand dollars per foot.

O'BRIEN: Rubbish. All the legal precedents are on our side.

WILLIE: That so? What about Fishbein versus the Empire State Building?

O'BRIEN: What about it?

WILLIE (*pointing at top shelf of law books*): You'll find it in Volume 16, New York Supplement Two, Page 45, 1939. A window-washer – sixty-first floor – the safety-belt broke – and whoosh! (*pantomimes a fall*)

THOMPSON: As window-washer, Mr. Fishbein was taking a normal occupational risk.

WILLIE: The window-washer's name was Jones. Mr. Fishbein was a pedestrian – walking innocently down 34th Street – and the next thing he knew, he was splattered all over the sidewalk. The widow sued – was awarded eighty-five thousand dollars. Case appealed, judgment upheld. (*pointing to law books*) Volume 259, Appellate Division, Page 56. Also Volume 24, New York Supplement Two, Page 168, 1940.

O'BRIEN: Maybe in New York they throw money around like that.

WILLLIE: All right. What about Mrs. Cunnigham versus Baltimore and Ohio Railroad – (*pointing to law books*) – U.S. District Court,

Eastern District of Ohio, Number 8927. Mrs. Cunnigham, en route to Cincinnati to visit dying uncle, gets trapped in the toilet on account of a faulty lock. The car is hitched to another train – Mrs. Cunnigham winds up in San Bernardino, California – by this time the uncle is dead – and she's cut out of the will. So she sues the railroad for damages. (*a beat*) Does this ring a bell?

THOMPSON: Never heard of it.

WILLIE (*looking around*): You mean *none* of you has? Because you gentlemen represented the railroad.

O'BRIEN: We did?

WILLIE: And lost the case.

O'BRIEN (*egg on his face*): Suppose we get back to the Hinkle case.

WILLIE: You guys should really bone up on negligence.

O'BRIEN (*picking up a file from his desk*): We've been going over the hospital report –

WILLIE: Discouraging, isn't it?

O'BRIEN: Naturally, we don't accept it at face value.

WILLIE: I wouldn't either.

THOMPSON: Look, Gingrich, let's stop horsing around. We demand the right to have our own doctors examine him.

WILLIE: You got it.

KINCAID: Unless you agree to it, we'll get a court order and force you.

WILLIE: I agree to it.

O'BRIEN: Now don't give us any trouble, Gingrich. We know your reputation. (*a delayed reaction*) What do you mean, you agree to it?

WILLIE: Permission granted.

THOMPSON: You have no objections?

WILLIE: As a matter of fact, I *insist* on it. To you gentlemen it's just a question of money – but to me, it's a personal tragedy – my kid brother-in-law – possibly disabled for life. I'm sure you'll bring in the best doctors – the kind of specialists we could never afford – maybe

you'll even send him to the Mayo Clinic.

O'BRIEN: Don't worry. Mr. Hinkle will get a thorough going-over.

WILLIE: Good. Will there be anything else, gentlemen?

O'BRIEN: I can't think of anything.

WILLIE: Well, I can. If you're to examine my client, you'll need written consent.

O'BRIEN: Yes, of course. (*to Thompson*) Get Miss Heffelfinger in here.

WILLIE: Don't bother. I've got the authorization right here. (*takes the papers out of his inside coat pocket*) Three copies – all signed and notarized. (*hands one to each partner*) Now if you'll excuse me, I have somebody waiting in my office. (*crosses to door, opens it, stops*) Interesting case. I'm considering suing the United Fruit Company. There should be a printed warning on every banana peel. Those things can be hazardous to your health. (*with a wave of his hand*) Carry on, gentlemen.

140

He exits, slamming the door. The draught knocks the ashes off the lawyers' cigars.

FADE.

5. The Chinese Lunch

19   INT. HOSPITAL ROOM – DAY

Harry is propped up in bed. By now he is encased in a steel and leather corset, which comes up under his chin and holds his head rigid. He is staring at the opposite wall, whence come the stirring sounds of THE BATTLE HYMN OF THE REPUBLIC, and a familiar voice.

VOICE: If you once forfeit the confidence of your fellow citizens, you can never regain their respect and esteem.

CAMERA DOLLIES BACK to include the TV set on the wall across the room. On the 11-inch screen is ABE LINCOLN, in stovepipe hat, with a shawl around his shoulders, addressing a crowd from the rear platform of a railroad car.

ABE: It is true that you may fool all the people some of the time – you can even fool some of the people all the time – but you can't fool all of the people all the time.

Harry mulls over this bit of homespun wisdom, as BATTLE HYMN OF THE REPUBLIC swells up on the sound track. The door opens and Willie comes in – hat, overcoat, and carrying a suitcase.

WILLIE: Hi, kid. What are you watching?

HARRY: An old movie about Abraham Lincoln.

He presses a button, switching off the set.

WILLIE: Lincoln? Great president. Lousy lawyer. *(puts the suitcase on the foot of the bed)* I picked up some stuff at your apartment – robe, slippers, your Playboy pajamas with the bunnies –

HARRY *(bitterly)*: How much longer do I have to stay here? Any rough idea?

WILLIE *(unpacking suitcase)*: It's just till the insurance doctors get through with your tests.

HARRY: I hope I flunk! I'm sick of pretending to doctors, and nurses, and mother and Charlotte –

WILLIE: You're not going to flunk. Take my word.

HARRY: Look at me. I can't sit up, I can't lie down, I can't sleep at night –

WILLIE: You'll get used to that corset.

HARRY: It's not the corset that's bugging me. Why did I let you talk me into this? Why?

Willie takes a silver-framed photograph out of the suitcase, hands it to him.

WILLIE: That's why.

It's a wedding picture. Harry and Sandy hurrying down the church steps, he in cutaway and striped pants, she in a white gown and veil, both of them laughing as they duck a shower of rice.

HARRY: Where did you find it?

WILLIE: Where you stashed it – on the top shelf of your closet – behind the 78 records.

He is putting the contents of the suitcase away in a bureau drawer.

HARRY *(studies photo with nostalgia)*: Remember that day? It was July Fourth. Some wise-guy put a firecracker under our bed.

WILLIE: Don't look at me. Check my son's alibi.

He has taken off his hat and overcoat, throws them on a chair. Harry sets the photo down on the night-table.

HARRY: Why hasn't she called yet? *(accusingly)* You said she'd call.

WILLIE: That's what *she* said. But it's only been a few days.

HARRY: Maybe she won't call at all.

WILLIE: Maybe she won't.

HARRY: What do you mean, she won't?

WILLIE: Maybe she's so anxious to see you that she's on a train right now – or a plane. Maybe that door will open and she'll just walk in.

There is a knock on the door. Harry looks at Willie, then at the door, then he lies back in bed.

HARRY (*in a weak voice*): Come in.

The door opens, and Mrs. Hinkle tiptoes in, followed by Charlotte. Mrs. Hinkle is carrying a thermos bottle, and a small straw basket covered with a napkin. As for Charlotte, she has now joined The Affluent Society. She is wearing a kit fox coat with a matching pillbox hat.

MRS HINKLE: Harry?

HARRY (*let down*): Hello, Mother. Hi, Charlotte.

MRS. HINKLE (*noticing Harry's harness*): My poor baby! What have they done to you? (*sobs*)

WILLIE (*matter-of-fact*): He's wearing a corset. Everybody wears a corset. You wear a corset, Charlotte wears a corset.

CHARLOTTE: I wear a girdle.

HARRY: Don't fight, please.

MRS. HINKLE: I brought you some mushroom soup and some hot biscuits.

WILLIE: Forget it. I ordered him a Chinese lunch.

HARRY: A Chinese lunch?

MRS. HINKLE: I spent all morning in the kitchen – (*a sob*)

HARRY: I'll have it for dinner.

WILLIE: Mother, you're upsetting everybody. You shouldn't be at the hospital – you should be in Florida. Four weeks in the sun –

MRS. HINKLE: Go away and leave Harry like that? I couldn't.

WILLIE: Don't worry. I'll take care of him. (*whips out a travel envelope from his pocket*) Here's the ticket. Your plane leaves tomorrow noon – I'll drive you to the airport in the new Mustang.

HARRY: What new Mustang?

WILLIE: *Your* new Mustang. But since you're in no condition to drive, I'm breaking it in for you.

HARRY: That's big of you.

WILLIE: What's your favorite color?

HARRY: Red.

WILLIE: Damn it! (*snaps his fingers*) I hope you don't mind – I got it in beige – to match Charlotte's fur coat.

HARRY: Oh?

His eyes travel to Charlotte. She turns slowly, modeling the coat.

CHARLOTTE: It's kit fox. The hat goes with it. You like it?

WILLIE: He loves it.

HARRY: Florida, and Mustangs and foxes – how are we paying for all this?

WILLIE: Our credit is good.

HARRY: Don't you think we better wait till we see some of that insurance money?

WILLIE: Wait? Who waits nowadays? Take the government – when they shoot a billion dollars'-worth of hardware into space – you think they pay cash? It's all on Diners' Club.

MRS. HINKLE (*suddenly noticing the wedding photo*) That terrible woman. What's she doing here?

WILLIE: If you must know – they're still crazy about each other.

MRS. HINKLE: Harry, you're not going to make the same mistake again? After what she did to you –

HARRY: Mother, why don't you go to Florida? Four weeks in the sun – baking your chest –

There is another knock on the door, and again Harry's hopes are aroused.

HARRY (*to Mrs. Hinkle, intensely*) Don't you insult her, Mother! (*calling off*) Come in.

The door opens. It's Boom Boom.

BOOM BOOM: Hi, buddy. How're you feeling?

HARRY (*let down again*): Oh. Come on in, Boom Boom.

BOOM BOOM: I brought you a present –

From the hallway he wheels in a sparkling new chrome wheel-chair, wrapped in cellophane, with a gay ribbon tied around it.

BOOM BOOM: – the boys on the team chipped in and we got you this.

HARRY: You shouldn't have.

At the sight of the wheel-chair, Mrs. Hinkle sobs.
BOOM BOOM: It's electric. It's got three speeds, left-hand drive, white sidewall tires, a safety-belt . . .
WILLIE (*eyeing it*): That's some chariot. Do they make a two-seater?
HARRY (*drily*): You already got a Mustang.
BOOM BOOM: And here's a little idea I had – *From his pocket he produces a bicycle horn with a rubber bulb on it.*
BOOM BOOM: You can mount it on the chair – and any time you need something –
He hoots the horn a couple of times. There are more sobs from Mrs. Hinkle. Boom Boom looks at her for a moment, agonized.
BOOM BOOM: Believe me, Mrs. Hinkle – instead of him needing that chair – I wish it was me.
MRS. HINKLE: If only they can make him walk again someday.
HARRY: I'll be fine, Mother.
WILLIE: Sure he will. Every week you read in Time Magazine how they're transplanting kidneys and making new spines out of fiberglass – don't you think the *doctors* read that stuff, too?
The door opens, and Sister Veronica comes in briskly, a clipboard in her hand.
SISTER VERONICA: Good morning. How's the patient? And how's the family?
WILLIE: Good morning, Sister.
As Sister Veronica crosses to the bed, she passes Boom Boom.
SISTER VERONICA (*under her breath*): Twelve and a half points, indeed! (*to Harry*) Here's the timetable for your insurance examinations this afternoon, by Professor Winterhalter and his staff.
HARRY: Professor?
SISTER VERONICA: He's Swiss, you know. (*consulting clipboard*) Two o'clock, electromyogram. Four o'clock, dynamometer test. Six o'clock, myelogram.
WILLIE: We'll be ready.

HARRY: We will?
SISTER VERONICA: Tomorrow is a real tough day – you start at seven in the morning. (*turns to Mrs. Hinkle, who is sobbing again*) Now, now, Mrs. Hinkle – we must be brave.
Willie gestures to Charlotte to get her out of there.
CHARLOTTE: Come on, Mother – I'll take you home and help you pack.
She and Sister Veronica lead Mrs. Hinkle toward the door.
MRS. HINKLE. Goodbye, Harry.
The door shuts after them. Boom Boom puts the bicycle horn on the bed beside Harry.

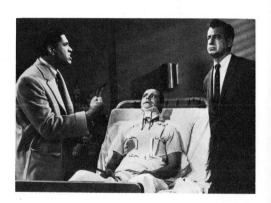

BOOM BOOM (*to Willie*): Why don't those insurance doctors leave him alone? Why do they put him through all this misery?
WILLIE: I don't blame them. There's big money involved – and you'd be surprised how many people try to fake a thing like this.
BOOM BOOM: Fake? (*a long look at Harry; then back to Willie, incensed*) They'd better have some empty beds around here – because if anybody calls my buddy a faker –
Harry, uncomfortable, picks up the bicycle horn with his left hand and honks it a couple of times.
HARRY: I used to have one like this on my bike.

BOOM BOOM: You want me to attach it now?
WILLIE: Later. (*easing him toward the door*) Let him get some rest.
BOOM BOOM: Sure.
HARRY: And thank the boys for the chair.
BOOM BOOM: That's okay, buddy. Use it in good health.
Willie shuts the door after him, crosses to the bed, all business.
WILLIE: Now let's get organized –
Harry looks grimly at the bicycle horn in his hand, suddenly tosses it across the room.
HARRY: I wish you'd tell him to stay away from here.
WILLIE: Why? He's a nice guy.
HARRY: That's what I mean.
He gets out of bed. Willie is consulting his watch.
WILLIE: Where's that Chinese lunch? (*sees Harry on his feet*) And what are you doing walking around?
HARRY: I'm trying to get some circulation in my legs. Do you mind?
WILLIE: Circulation? That's the last thing we want. Now why don't we just get back in bed –
HARRY: What is this with the *we*?
WILLIE: We're in this together – you and I – straight down the line – fifty-fifty.
HARRY: Fifty-fifty?
WILLIE: Don't you think that's fair? I'm devoting ninety percent of my time to this case. And if *you* louse it up, *we* lose the case, and *I* get nothing.
There is a knock on the door. Harry jumps back into bed. Willie opens the door, revealing the ferret-faced nurse.
WILLIE: Yes?
NURSE: Did you order some lunch sent in?
WILLIE: Yeah – right here.
The nurse ushers in a shrivelled man of sixty, in hat and overcoat, carrying a loaded tray covered with a napkin. His name is SCHINDLER.
WILLIE (*to Schindler*): What the hell took you so long? A slow boat from China? We got a

hungry man here.
NURSE (*to Schindler*): He talks to me like that all the time.
She has wheeled up a small utility table to the bed, and Schindler sets the tray down on it.
HARRY: I don't want any food.
Willie whips the napkin away, starts removing the plastic covers from the dishes.
WILLIE: Look at this. Fried shrimp – egg rolls – chicken chow mein –
HARRY: And I certainly don't want any *Chinese* food.
WILLIE (*to Schindler*): Tea – where's the tea – you forgot the tea! (*snapping his fingers*) Nurse, get us a pot of tea.
NURSE: *Please?*
WILLIE: Please.
NURSE: That's more like it.
She exits. Harry, meanwhile, has been casing the food.
HARRY: Maybe I'll just have an egg roll.
He picks one up, but before it reaches his mouth, Willie slaps it out of his hand.
WILLIE: Put that down. Okay, let's go, Schindler.
Schindler uncovers another plate, revealing a most peculiar oriental delicacy – a hypodermic needle and some ampules.
HARRY: What's that? (*to Willie*) And don't tell me it's chop suey.
WILLIE: He's going to give you a shot – to help you pass those tests.
HARRY: Oh, no. I'm not taking any shots from a *waiter*.
WILLIE: What do you mean, waiter? This is Doc Schindler, from Chicago.
SCHINDLER: Howdy.
WILLIE: Those insurance guys – they think they're such geniuses. What they forget is that everytime they build a better mousetrap, the mice get smarter, too.
Schindler has picked up the hypodermic and an ampule.

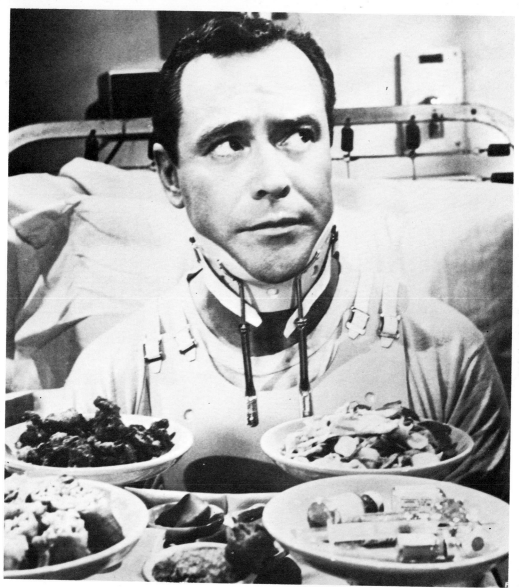

HARRY: You'll be careful, won't you, Doc?

SCHINDLER: I better be – because I'm on parole.

HARRY: Parole?

SCHINDLER: They caught me tampering with a horse at Arlington Park.

HARRY (*to Willie*): A *veterinary*?

WILLIE: Well, actually, he's a dentist.

SCHINDLER: Where do you want it?

WILLIE: Right arm and left leg. Make 'em good and numb.

SCHINDLER: Oh, *numb*!

WILLIE: Sure, We want those nerves blocked.

SCHINDLER: Then I better use the Novocain.

Because with *this* stuff, he'll run the mile in 1:34 flat.

He squirts the liquid out of of the syringe, picks up another ampule.

HARRY: I just hope they don't give me a saliva test.

WILLIE: Step on it, Doc. We still got Sam the Hypnotist coming.

HARRY: Sam the *who*?

WILLIE: Just a little post-hypnotic suggestion – you're going to have such symptoms like you wouldn't believe.

Schindler, the hypodermic poised, rolls up

Harry's right sleeve.
WILLIE: Find a nice freckle – so the puncture won't show.
SCHINDLER: All rightie . . . now just relax.
HARRY: OW!
WILLIE: That's the boy.
Schindler has now withdrawn the needle, and Harry is rubbing his arm, grimacing.
HARRY: What if I get an infection from this?
WILLIE: So we sue the hospital – for using dirty needles. (to Schindler) Now the leg.
Schindler moves to the left side of the bed, starts digging under the covers. Willie crosses to the door, opens it slightly, peeks out into the corridor.
WIILLIE (over his shoulder): Hurry up! Here comes the nurse!
SCHINDLER: I'm looking for a freckle. (he ducks his head under the covers)
There is an OW! from off-scene as the nurse comes through the door with a cup of tea.
NURSE: I used my influence in the kitchen.
She reaches the bed just as Schindler is withdrawing his head from under the covers, hiding the hypodermic behind his back. The nurse gives him an odd look.
WILLIE: We lost a shrimp somewhere.
He quickly removes the dish with the ampules from the tray. The nurse holds the teacup out to Harry. He waves it away.
HARRY: I don't want it. Take it away. Take *everything* away.
NURSE: Everything?
HARRY: You eat it.
NURSE: Don't you even want the fortune cookie? Come on – you've got to open your fortune cookie.
She hands him the fortune cookie. He crushes it with his left hand, looks at the slip of paper inside, reacts.
WILLIE: What does it say?
HARRY (reading): You can fool all the people some of the time, and some of the people all the time –

WILLIE (is Harry pulling his leg?) Let me see that!
He grabs the slip of paper, checks it – that's exactly what it says. He crumples the paper up, tosses it away in disgust.
WILLIE: Those Chinese! What do *they* know?
FADE.

6. The Snake Pit

20   A MONTAGE OF EXAMINATIONS
Harry is being put through a series of exhaustive tests by four impressive-looking DOCTORS. *Supervizing the proceedings is* PROFESSOR WINTERHALTER, *who almost won the Nobel Prize in* 1926.

A.   THE ELECTROMYOGRAM TEST –
Harry is lying on a table, with two wires running from his wrists and ankles into two machines equipped with oscilloscopes and loud-speakers. Light impulses streak across the little screens, accompanied by beeping sounds.
The four doctors are hovering over Harry, while Prof. Winterhalter, the monocle in his eye, is studying the oscilloscopes.
FIRST DOCTOR (extending thumb toward Harry's right hand): Squeeze! (Harry squeezes)
SECOND DOCTOR (pressing back the big toe of Harry's left foot): Push! (Harry pushes)
THIRD DOCTOR (running tailor's wheel down Harry's left arm): Feel this?
HARRY: Yes.
FOURTH DOCTOR (hits tuning fork, holds it against Harry's right knee): How about this?
HARRY: E-flat?
The first doctor has crossed to the machines, switches them off.
FIRST DOCTOR: Well, gentlemen, the evidence seems to be quite clear.
SECOND DOCTOR: There are obvious indications of nerve trauma.

THIRD DOCTOR: Obviously.

FOURTH DOCTOR: I concur.

FIRST DOCTOR: And what is your learned opinion, Professor Winterhalter?

PROF. WINTERHALTER: I have not formulated an opinion yet. But I have formulated a hunch –

HARRY (hopefully): Oh?

PROF. WINTERHALTER: FAKE! (the monocle drops out of his eye)

HARRY (deflated): Oh.

B. THE DYNAMOMETER TEST – Start on a magnifying glass, held against Harry's right arm – the spot where Doc Schindler has injected the Novocain. CAMERA PULLS BACK. It is Prof. Winterhalter who is looking through the glass very suspiciously.

HARRY (feebly): It's a freckle.

Prof. Winterhalter turns away, eyebrows arched. The first doctor hands Harry a dynamometer.

FIRST DOCTOR: Pull! (Harry pulls with his left hand) Left hand, 45 – (Harry pulls with his right hand) – right hand, 2.

SECOND DOCTOR: Two? There is a pronounced discrepancy in the reflexes.

THIRD DOCTOR: Indubitably.

FOURTH DOCTOR: We seem to be confronted with a classic syndrome.

FIRST DOCTOR: Wouldn't you say so, Professor Winterhalter?

Prof. Winterhalter, who has been cleaning his monocle, inserts it in his eye.

PROF. WINTERHALTER: I once zaw a zimilar case in Zurich.

HARRY (hopefully): Oh?

PROF. WINTERHALTER: Also FAKE!

HARRY (deflated): Oh!

C. THE MYELOGRAM TEST – This is a fluoroscope job. The room is darkened, Harry is lying on his stomach on a table. The specialists, in leather aprons and tinted goggles, are clustered around the fluoroscope, studying the flow of dye that has been injected in Harry's back.

FIRST DOCTOR: Fascinating, isn't it, the way we can now corroborate subjective symptoms.

SECOND DOCTOR (to third Doctor): It's a new technique they developed in Rochester.

THIRD DOCTOR: I know. I read all about it in Time Magazine.

The first doctor tilts up the fluoroscope, while the fourth doctor switches on the lights.

FIRST DOCTOR: Well, gentlemen, I think we must agree that our findings are not inconsistent with the exacerbation of the median nerve and the lumbar plexus.

The four doctors are now removing their goggles.

SECOND DOCTOR: I agree.

THIRD DOCTOR: So do I.

FOURTH DOCTOR: Are we then unanimous in our evaluation, Professor Winterhalter?

Prof. Winterhalter turns his face into CAMERA. Again there is a monocle in his eye – but this time it is made of dark glass.

PROF. WINTERHALTER (booming): FAKE!

Harry reacts. Prof. Winterhalter removes his monocle and gestures with it.

PROF. WINTERHALTER: All these new-fangled machines – fake! They prove nothing! In the old days, we used to do these things better. A man says he is paralyzed, you simply throw him in the snake pit. If he climbs out, then you know he is lying.

FIRST DOCTOR: And if he doesn't climb out?

PROF. WINTERHALTER: Then we have lost a patient – but we have found an honest man!

Harry, who has been listening with growing apprehension, is now on the verge of panic.

HARRY: Wait a minute, you guys. You're not throwing me in any pit! And you bring one snake in here – just one little snake – (a cry for help) WILLIE!

FADE.

7 The Gemini Plan

21 INT. O'BRIEN'S OFFICE – DAY

Here they are again – O'Brien behind the desk, Thompson, Kincaid and Mr. Purkey sitting in a half-circle facing him.

O'BRIEN (*reading from report*): . . . Therefore, to answer the most vital question – is the patient indeed disabled, or is he merely simulating? After an analysis in depth of all the diagnostic data, we, the undersigned doctors, have come to the definite conclusion that the evidence is definitely inconclusive! . . . Enclosed please find a bill for our services and a detailed list of our expenses – (*throws the report aside, in disgust*) Double-talk! Thirty-seven hundred dollars'-worth of double-talk!

THOMPSON: You know, this case has been getting a lot of publicity. Maybe we could save the insurance company some money if we just settled.

O'BRIEN: Settle? A phony claim? Never! It's not just their money that's at stake, it's our integrity! If we let shysters like Gingrich ride roughshod over the laws of this land – (*breaks off, deflating*) All right. (*picks up phone*) Get Gingrich on the phone.

22 INT. GINGRICH OFFICE – DAY

A tailor is fitting a blue pin-stripe Italian suit on Willie. Also in evidence are a black chesterfield, a Homburg in a hat-box, and a couple of boxes of monogrammed shirts. The tailor is stooped over, measuring Willie's trouser leg.

TAILOR: You wear a belt or suspenders?

WILLIE: Suspenders? They went out with Clarence Darrow. Great Lawyer. Lousy dresser. (*the phone rings; he picks it up*) Hello? Gingrich here . . . Yes, Mr. O'Brien. That's all right – I just have my tailor here – I'm too busy to get away from the office.

23 INT. O'BRIEN'S OFFICE – DAY

O'Brien is on the phone, his partners and Purkey watching him.

O'BRIEN: We know you're a busy man, Gingrich – and we're pretty busy, too – so why bother with something as trifling as this Hinkle case? It may drag through the courts for months. What I mean is – we wouldn't be averse to discussing a settlement.

24 INT. GINGRICH OFFICE – DAY

Willie has the phone to his ear, but is covering the mouthpiece with his hand.

WILLIE (*to tailor*): I'd like to have a matching tie and handkerchief – nothing flashy – maybe something like this.

He opens his coat to reveal the lining – blue polka dots on a white ground.

WILLIE (*into phone*): Sorry, You were saying?

25 INT. O'BRIEN'S OFFICE – DAY

O'BRIEN (*into phone*): In return for a release from all future claims, we are willing to compensate your client with a lump sum – say, two thousand dollars. Fair enough?

26 INT. GINGRICH OFFICE – DAY

WILLIE (*into phone*): It may be fair – but it's not enough. I had a slightly different figure in mind – say, five hundred thousand?

27 INT. O'BRIEN'S OFFICE – DAY

O'BRIEN (*into phone*): Five hundred thousand? (*a reaction from the other partners*) You're being grotesque! (*boiling over*) Let me tell you something, Gingrich – as one member of the Bar to another – if indeed you are a member of the Bar –

28 INT. GINGRICH OFFICE – DAY

The tailor is removing Willie's coat, and as he talks, Willie switches the phone from one hand to the other, to accommodate him.

WILLIE: Look, Mr. O'Brien, I don't want to be unreasonable. You say two thousand – I say five hundred thousand – tell you what – let's split it down the middle.

29 INT. O'BRIEN'S OFFICE – DAY
O'Brien, his blood pressure sky-high, slams the receiver down.

O'BRIEN: All right! If he wants a knockdown fight, we'll give it to him! And no compromise!

KINCAID: I'm with you.

THOMPSON: Now wait a minute. (*picks up medical report*) We can't go in front of a jury with *this* kind of evidence.

O'BRIEN: We're not in front of a jury yet. Purkey, I want you to put Hinkle under surveillance.

PURKEY: I was about to suggest that.

O'BRIEN: He can't keep up this act much longer – sooner or later he's bound to crack.

PURKEY: He's getting out of the hospital to-morrow. Shall we proceed with our standard operation?

O'BRIEN: What's that?

PURKEY: Microphone – tape recorder – eight millimeter camera – daytime coverage.

O'BRIEN: And at night he can go out dancing? No, sir! We have to do better than that.

PURKEY: In that case, may I recommend our Gemini Plan?

O'BRIEN: What's Gemini?

PURKEY: Two operatives – twenty-four hour coverage – a microphone in every room – 16-millimeter camera – telescopic lens – and Technicolor!   FADE.

8. The Torch

30 INT. HOSPITAL ROOM – DAY
A pale, drawn Harry is dressed for departure – suit, corset, duffel coat. He is sitting in his wheel-chair – the safety-belt fastened, the bicycle horn now attached to the left arm-rest – staring moodily out the window at the gray winter morning. On the bed, three-quarters packed, is his suitcase. From the bathroom comes Boom Boom's voice, humming 'Wave the Flag'.
Boom Boom comes out carrying Harry's robe and pajamas, puts them in the suitcase. Harry doesn't look at him. Boom Boom returns to the bathroom, singing all the while. Harry honks the horn sharply, and Boom Boom reappears with the toilet kit in his hand.

BOOM BOOM: What is it, buddy? You want something?

HARRY (*tense*): Yeah. I want you to cut out that singing.

BOOM BOOM: Sorry. (*looking around*) Let's see, have we got everything? . . . Oh, yes – slippers. *Picks them up from under the bed, tosses them in the suitcase.*

HARRY: Shouldn't you be at the stadium – practicing with the team?

BOOM BOOM: So I'm AWOL. But the way I figure, I put you in here – the least I can do is help you move out.

HARRY: Look, Boom Boom – I don't want you to get into any trouble on account of me.

BOOM BOOM: So they fine me another hundred bucks. Big deal.

HARRY: What do you mean – *another* hundred?

BOOM BOOM: I walked out on the coaching session last Tuesday – just couldn't take it – I went to a neighborhood bar and had a couple of beers.

HARRY: Couldn't take what?

BOOM BOOM: They were running the film of the Vikings game – and when it came to – our accident – they had it in slow motion –

Upset all over again, he looks away from Harry, spots Dr. Schindler's chopsticks on the night-table.

BOOM BOOM: You want these chopsticks?

HARRY: To hell with them.

Boom Boom tosses the chopsticks aside, picks up the framed wedding photo from the night-table, looks at it.

BOOM BOOM: I don't mean to be personal – but didn't you say your wife was coming to see you?

HARRY: She's dead.

BOOM BOOM: Oh?

HARRY: As far as I'm concerned. So don't pack that picture.

They are not aware that Willie has now appeared in the doorway, and is standing there listening. It's a spruced-up Willie – the old tweed coat is gone, and he is wearing the chesterfield and the Homburg.

BOOM BOOM (*to Harry, holding up photo*): Well – what do you want me to do with it?

HARRY: Toss it out the window – flush it down the drain – who cares?

Willie advances into the room.

WILLIE: Don't you even want to save the

152

frame? (*Harry wheels himself around to face him*) We're all checked out. Ready to go, kid?

HARRY (*boiling inside*): Not before I talk to my lawyer.

WILLIE (*sensing trouble; to Boom Boom*): What kind of car are you driving?

BOOM BOOM: A Caddie. Why?

WILLIE: I don't think we can get him *and* the wheel-chair into the Mustang.

BOOM BOOM: No sweat, I'll bring my car around to the front entrance.

He exits.

CHARLOTTE: Charlotte has fixed up mother's room for you.

HARRY (*sarcastic*): That's nice.

WILLIE: You'll be better off staying with us – helpless as you are. (*Harry unbuckles the safety-belt, gets to his feet*) Watch it! Somebody may walk through that door any minute.

HARRY: You bet. And it's going to be me.

WILLIE: Harry –

HARRY: I'm walking out of here on my own two feet – and without this damn corset –

He removes his coat, starts to untie his corset.

WILLIE: Are you crazy? After all we've gone through? We've got them over a barrel now – they're already trying to settle –

HARRY (*pointing toward door where Boom Boom exited*): You see the way that guy looks at me? I'm going to let him off the hook.

WILLIE: Harry, you walk out of here and they'll get you for fraud!

HARRY: Let 'em!

WILLIE: How can you be so selfish? What about all the money I've been spending?

HARRY: You'll think of something.

WILLIE: I *did* think of something – but you're fighting it. What's the matter – you afraid of a little prosperity? You're hopeless, Harry. A loser! Always have been, always will be. A guy who jumps off roofs with a closed umbrella! (*the phone is ringing now, and he grabs it*) Yeah? . . . Hold on. (*covering mouthpiece, to Harry*)

A born loser! You want to know why you lost your wife? Because you got no character – no guts. I'm surprised it didn't show up in the X-rays.

HARRY: You left out the most important thing – no brains! Buying all that bull about how I was going to get Sandy back. Well, I don't want any part of her – not any more. The cold-blooded little tramp – shacked up with that guy there –

WILLIE: Not so loud. You want her to hear? (*he holds up the phone*) It's Sandy. (*Harry doesn't move*) Shall I hang up? (*Harry takes a*

step toward the phone) Get back in that chair! *Harry obediently goes back to the wheel-chair. Willie shoots him a smug look.*

WILLIE (*into phone*): Yes, Sandy? . . . He's coming along all right – he has his bad spells once in a while – but the doctors think he'll walk again.

31   INT. NEW YORK APARTMENT
Sandy is propped up in bed, phone in hand, a cigarette in her mouth. The door to the bathroom is ajar, and a man's silhouette can be seen against the shower curtain. Sandy is again speaking in an undertone, and occasionally throws a furtive look toward the bathroom.

SANDY (*into phone*): Poor bastard. I just hope he winds up with a little money. But with you handling the case, I know he will.

32   INT. HOSPITAL ROOM
Harry has now wheeled himself up beside Willie.
WILLIE (*into phone*): Don't worry. If he had as good a doctor as he has a legal adviser – (*Harry is trying to get the phone away from him*) Here he is. (*hands him the phone*)
HARRY (*into phone; controlling his eagerness*) Hello, Sandy . . . Yes, it's me. Why are you so surprised?

33   INT. NEW YORK APARTMENT
SANDY (*into phone*): Well, I only called Willie to find out how you were. I didn't really think you'd want to talk to me ever again – the way you sounded last time.

34   INT. HOSPITAL ROOM
HARRY (*into phone*): It was right after the accident – I was full of sedatives – I didn't know what I was saying . . .
Willie leans against the wall, lights a cigarette, never taking his eyes off Harry.
HARRY (*into phone*): Well, I'm being discharged from the hospital today – I guess there's nothing

more they can do for me here.

35 INT. NEW YORK APARTMENT

SANDY (*into phone*): Where are you going to go?
. . . Sure I care . . . From what Willie says, I
suppose you can't get around very well.

36 INT. HOSPITAL ROOM

HARRY (*into phone*): Don't listen to him. Just
because I'm in a corset and a wheel-chair – you
learn to live with those things . . . As a matter of
fact, Willie wants me to move in with them –
but I don't like to impose on anybody. I figure
I'll just go back to the apartment – you
remember our old apartment?

37 INT. NEW YORK APARTMENT

SANDY (*into phone; warmly*): Of course I do . . .
You still have that ugly brown velveteen
couch?
*The shower goes off. She glances toward the
bathroom, slides out of bed, carries the phone out
into the kitchen, talking all the while in a muted
voice.*
SANDY (*into phone*): And those two sets of
mother-of-pearl demi-tasse spoons we got for a
wedding present? . . . And that cat – what was
her name – Tinker Bell?

38 INT. HOSPITAL ROOM

HARRY (*into phone*): Everything's the same –
except the cat. She ran away, too. There must
be something the matter with me.

39 INT. NEW YORK APARTMENT

SANDY (*into phone*): Don't say that. Maybe
there's something the matter with Tinker Bell.
(*a long beat*): Harry, I was wondering – who's
going to look after you?

40 INT. HOSPITAL ROOM

HARRY (*into phone*): Oh, I'll manage somehow.
Of course, it may be a little frustrating in the

beginning – and a little lonely.
*Behind his back, Willie very casually picks up
the wedding photo from the bed, puts it into the
suitcase.*
HARRY (*into phone*): No, mother's in Florida.
But maybe Charlotte will drop by and bring me
some mushroom soup – and I can get myself a
babysitter once in a while –

41 INT. NEW YORK APARTMENT

SANDY (*into phone*): Harry – do you want me to
come and sit with you? . . . Just say yes or no.

42 INT. HOSPITAL ROOM

Willie is now snapping up Harry's corset.
HARRY (*into phone*): Naturally the answer is yes.
It's always nice to see an old roommate . . . but
if it's in any way awkward – I don't know what
your situation is – and I don't want to make any
difficulties for you . . .

43 INT. NEW YORK APARTMENT

SANDY (*into phone*): Let me handle that . . .
What if I can get away for a few days?
MAN'S VOICE (*from bathroom*): Sandy! (*a wet,
naked arm appears through the opening in the
door*) There's no towels!
SANDY (*covering phone*): Coming. (*into phone;
an urgent whisper*) All right then – see you
Monday. And take care of yourself, do you
hear?
She puts the receiver down carefully.

44 INT. HOSPITAL ROOM

*Harry, transported, still holds the phone in his
hand. Willie is draping the duffel coat around his
shoulders.*
HARRY (*into phone*): Loud and clear! (*hangs up;
to Willie*) Guess what?
WILLIE: Tinker Bell is coming back?
*Harry nods happily. Boom Boom appears in the
doorway.*
BOOM BOOM: I got the car out front. All set?

HARRY (*jubilant*): You bet. Let's blow this joint. (*wheels himself around*) Out of my way!
Boom Boom just manages to step aside as Harry whizzes past him. Honking his horn, he makes a sharp turn into the corridor.
BOOM BOOM (*calling after him*): Hey, fasten your seat belt. Those things go eight miles an hour.
Willie has shut the suitcase. He picks it up, heads for the door.

45 FOURTH FLOOR – HOSPITAL
Harry, singing 'Wave the Flag' at the top of his voice, guns the wheel-chair down the corridor, weaving in and out among nurses, patients, interns and nuns. He reaches the elevator just as the door opens and scoots inside, almost running down Sister Veronica, who is stepping out. She looks after him as Willie, carrying the suitcase, and Boom Boom come up.
SISTER VERONICA (*to Willie, with a broad grin*): Doesn't it do your heart good? I have a hunch he'll be up and around in no time.
WILLIE: Now look, Sister – I asked you to pray for him – but we don't want any miracles!
He and Boom Boom step into the elevator and the door slides shut.   FADE.

9. The Whirlpool

46 EAST 20TH STREET – A COLD WINTRY DAY
It's a middle-class street in mid-town Cleveland. There is an apartment house on one side of the street, and the classiest thing about it is Boom Boom's white Cadillac parked in front of the entrance. Across the street is a rundown building with a sign reading: ROOMS BY DAY OR WEEK.
CAMERA STARTS ON a bay window on the second floor of the apartment house. This is
Harry Hinkle's pad. After a moment the CAMERA WHIPS ACROSS THE STREET and converges on a window of the rooming house. The window is open from the bottom, and a dirty shade is drawn. Through a round hole cut in the blind protrudes a telescopic lens.

47 INT. DETECTIVE'S ROOM – DAY
The Gemini Plan is in operation, all systems go. Purkey is sitting on the single brass bed in the small, dingy room. He wears a pair of earphones, plugged into a tape-recorder whirring away on the night-table. Mounted on a tripod is a 16-millimeter camera, aimed through the hole in the shade. Slouched in a chair beside it is the cameraman, a youngish wise-guy named MAX. He is reading Ian Fleming's THUNDERBALL, soft-cover. It is cold in the room, and they are both wearing their coats, hats, and gloves.
Purkey, with a puzzled frown, removes the earphones. Out of them comes faintly Boom Boom's voice: 'One, two – one, two – one, two – left, right – left, right – '
PURKEY (*to Max*): What's that with the one-two, left-right? (*Max continues reading*) Hey, Max! (*snaps his fingers*) What are they doing over there? Can you see anything?
Max puts down the book, peers through the finder.
MAX (*a beat*): They're dancing the Frug.
PURKEY: What?
He rushes to the camera, shoves Max aside, looks through the finder.

48 EXT. APARTMENT HOUSE – SECOND STORY WINDOW – DAY
Through the finder, with its crossed hairs, he sees into Harry's living room. Harry, wearing his corset, slacks and slippers, is on his feet, holding on to a walker. Boom Boom, a towel around his neck, is across the room, encouraging Harry to come toward him. Harry takes a couple of painful steps, stops.

49   INT. DETECTIVES' ROOM – DAY

Purkey turns away from the camera, looks at Max, disgusted.

PURKEY: The Frug! Some sense of humor.

MAX: If you ask me, we're just wasting our time. I think this guy is legit.

PURKEY: Maybe so. But let's give it a chance.

MAX: We've been watching for three days and three nights. That colored guy, he has to dress him, shave him, feed him, put him to bed, carry him to the toilet, brush his teeth – if that's an act, then I'm Soupy Sales.

PURKEY: Listen, I once shadowed a guy who was suing the Yellow Cab Company – some kind of collision – claimed he was paralyzed. For six weeks we were watching him and nothing – never even moved a muscle – he had this Swedish masseuse come every so often and give him a rubdown. Then one night, Bingo! – there he was giving *her* a rubdown.

MAX: No kidding.

PURKEY: Caught him red-handed. Except that idiot cameraman – he got so carried away – he forgot to roll the film.

MAX: Couldn't you ask for another take?

PURKEY: Mind if I laugh after lunch? (*indicating earphones*) Keep an ear on them. I'm going down to the drugstore.

He starts toward the door.

MAX: Bring me back a corned beef on rye, hold the butter, easy on the mustard, and a strawberry milk-shake.

PURKEY: Anything else?

MAX: A pack of Tiparillos.

Purkey exits, slamming the door. Max clamps the earphones to his head.

50   INT. HARRY HINKLE'S APARTMENT – DAY

There is a living room with a bay window giving on the street. A swinging door leads to the kitchen, and an archway leads to the bedroom and bathroom. The place is neat and comfortable, the furniture is a mixture of Grand Rapids and Hand-Me-Down. There are books, records, a stereo phonograph, a 16-inch TV, that ugly brown velveteen couch, and a framed reproduction of Whistler's Mother on the wall.

Harry, clinging to the walker, has laboriously made his way across the room to within a few feet of Boom Boom.

BOOM BOOM: Left right – left, right – go, man, go! – just a couple of more steps –

An exhausted Harry makes those two final steps.

BOOM BOOM: Attaboy!

He picks Harry up in his arms, carries him over to the wheel-chair, sets him down.

BOOM BOOM: You're doing great. (*wipes the sweat from Harry's face with the towel*) I've been talking to the guys in the front office – we want you to be at the stadium November 27th.

HARRY: What's November 27th?

BOOM BOOM: Night game – against Washington – we'd like to make it Harry Hinkle night.

HARRY: Oh, no.

BOOM BOOM: You just sit on the bench with the team – and then at half-time, they introduce you, and you make a little speech –

HARRY: No, thank you, Boom Boom. I'd rather not.

He turns away in embarrassment. His eyes fall on a vase of flowers standing on the end table.

HARRY (*changing the subject*): Don't you think those flowers would be better over there?

He points to the TV set. Boom Boom picks up the flowers, carries them to the TV set, puts them down beside the framed wedding photo.

BOOM BOOM (*looking at Sandy in the photo*): What time is the plane due?

HARRY: Three-forty – United Airlines. (*he takes a telegram from his left pants pocket; reads*) Coming in on a wing and a prayer. Love, Sandy.

BOOM BOOM: I sure hope she likes my dinner.

HARRY: What're we having?

BOOM BOOM: Chicken.

HARRY: Fried chicken?

BOOM BOOM: No. Chicken paprika – with red cabbage – and for dessert, apricot dumplings.

HARRY: What kind of food is that?

BOOM BOOM: It's Hungarian. I learned it from my mother.

HARRY: Your mother?

BOOM BOOM: She used to work as a cook in a Hungarian restaurant.

HARRY: Oh?

Boom Boom carries the walker through the archway into the bedroom. There are twin beds with a night-table between them. One of the beds is made up, on the other there are just a bare mattress and a bare pillow.

BOOM BOOM: You want me to fix up the other bed?

HARRY (*a beat*): I really don't know – I mean, how long she's going to stay, or what her plans are, or – (*another beat*) Go ahead. Make it up.

BOOM BOOM. Why not? What have we got to lose?

He takes some linen out of a chest-of-drawers. Harry wheels himself over to the record cabinet, starts to search for a record.

HARRY: You ever been married, Boom Boom?

BOOM BOOM: No. But I'm engaged to a girl in Detroit.

HARRY: You are?

BOOM BOOM: And a girl in Baltimore – and one in Green Bay, Wisconsin – and *two* in San Francisco –

HARRY: Hold it! When you say engaged – you mean you give *each* of them a ring?

BOOM BOOM: Sure, The minute the team hits town.

HARRY: Funny thing about marriage – it's like being in the army – everybody knocks it – but you'd be surprised how many guys re-enlist.

By this time he has found the record he was looking for – it's an acetate dub in a plain brown sleeve. He puts the record on the turn-table, switches it on. A small band is playing Cole

Porter's YOU'D BE SO NICE TO COME HOME TO. Harry listens for a moment, then wheels himself over to the bedroom arch. By now Boom Boom has put the bottom sheet on the mattress. He unfolds the top sheet, tosses it across the bed with an expert flourish.

HARRY (*watching him*): Where did you learn that? (*before Boom Boom can answer*) Don't tell me – your father was a Pullman porter.

BOOM BOOM (*shaking his head*): He was a fighter. Light-heavyweight. Once went twelve rounds with Billy Conn.

HARRY: Say!

BOOM BOOM: He was really going places. Then he killed a guy in the ring – blood-clot or something. He never fought again after that. Just started hitting the bottle.

HARRY: That's a shame.

BOOM BOOM: He pulled out okay – as a matter of fact, we're in business together – I bought this bowling alley on the East Side – and he's running it for me. It's got twelve lanes and a cocktail bar, and it's half paid off. All I need is another three good seasons of pro ball.

HARRY (*concerned*): Boom Boom – what happened to you yesterday?

BOOM BOOM (*innocently*): Yesterday?

HARRY: I watched the game on television.

BOOM BOOM (*shrugging*): I guess I wasn't very sharp – so they benched me. Anybody can have a bad afternoon.

HARRY (*looking straight at him*): You're not drinking, are you?

BOOM BOOM: Me? No, Sir. Maybe a beer now and then – but I can't take the hard stuff.

He starts to put a blanket on the bed. From the phonograph now comes a female voice singing the chorus of YOU'D BE SO NICE TO COME HOME TO. Harry listens for a moment.

HARRY: You know who that is? Sandy.

BOOM BOOM (*moving into living room*): I didn't know she was a singer.

HARRY (*with a wry smile*): She always wanted

to be. That was our problem. When we were first married, she was working at WJW – doing singing commercials for a linoleum company. There was this band – Gus Gilroy and His Gaslighters – she cut an audition record with them – and the next thing I knew, she'd run off to New York with that Gilroy character. She was going to make it big.

BOOM BOOM: Did she?

HARRY: If she did, the news hasn't reached Cleveland. (*the record comes to an end*) For a year now, I've tried very hard to get her out of my mind – I worked at it day and night – because I figured I'd never see her again. Just imagine – right now she's stepping on a plane in New York – and in a few minutes, she'll take off.

Joyously, he *takes off in the wheel-chair, circling and swooping around the room in an improvized dance, humming YOU'D BE SO NICE TO COME HOME TO. Boom Boom watches him with amusement.*

51   EXT. EAST 20TH STREET – DAY
A brand new tan, fastback Mustang drives up and stops behind Boom Boom's Cadillac. The driver is Willie, in chesterfield and Homburg. Humming the overture to 'The Barber of Seville', he takes an attaché case from the seat beside him, and is about to get out of the car, when suddenly he sees something that makes him freeze.
On the sidewalk across the street, Purkey is approaching the rooming house, carrying an open cardboard box with Max's lunch.
In the Mustang, Willie pulls back slightly, watches Purkey enter the rooming house. Then he glances up the façade of the building, wondering what Purkey is up to. He opens the door of the car, steps out, hurries into the apartment house.

52   INT. HARRY'S APARTMENT – DAY
Harry, still humming and waltzing around in the wheel-chair, is just heading into the kitchen

when the doorbell rings, Boom Boom crosses to the door, opens it. It's Willie.

BOOM BOOM: Hi, Mr. Gingrich.

WILLIE: Hello, Boomsy.

He looks around. Harry reappears from the kitchen, circles around him.

WILLIE: Hey, Nureyev – you're going to wear out your batteries. (*Harry ignores him*) Now cut that out! You're not a well man!

Harry stops. Willie puts his attaché case and Homburg down on an end table.

HARRY: I've been trying to reach you all morning. Where have you been?

WILLIE: Where have I been? Working. Talking to witnesses – getting depositions – looking out for your interests.

He turns his back to the window, takes out a gold cigarette case, opens it, removes a cigarette.

WILLIE: I've interviewed every person who was sitting between the twenty- and forty-yard lines – gotten signed statements from the groundspeakers – looked at miles of TV tape – instant replays – isolated camera.

He manipulates the cigarette case in his hand till he catches a reflection on the inside of the lid. It is the window of the rooming house across the street, with the telescopic lens protruding through the shade. He snaps the case shut, starts wandering around the room, looking for hidden mikes.

WILLIE: In this business, you got to be on your toes every minute – thinking – anticipating – always keeping one step ahead of the other guy.

He picks up the cushions of the couch, examines a lamp on the end table.

HARRY: I thought you could pick up Sandy at the airport. She's arriving at three-forty.

WILLIE: Good for you! I can't wait to see that pretty puss around again here (*lighting cigarette*) Why doesn't Boom Boom pick her up?

HARRY: Boom Boom?

BOOM BOOM: Be glad to.

WILLIE (*moving around room*): Three-forty –

breaks up the whole afternoon – and there are some important things I have to take care of.

HARRY (*indicating Boom Boom*): He doesn't even know what she looks like.

BOOM BOOM (*smiling*): Don't worry. I won't bring you the wrong wife.

Willie has now spotted a wire running along the floorboard. His eyes follow it to the radiator and there, hanging between the radiator pipes, is a microphone.

WILLIE: Sure is nice and warm here. (*crosses to radiator*)

HARRY: Yeah. Somebody came up from the building and checked the radiators in every room.

WILLIE (*removing his coat*): Every room. H'mmm! Isn't that considerate?

53   INT. DETECTIVES' ROOM – DAY

Max, sitting beside the camera, is eating his sandwich. Purkey, listening on the earphones, frowns worriedly.

PURKEY: I think they suspect something! (*Max looks through the finder*) I told you not to plant those mikes in the radiators.

MAX (*turning to him*): I suppose your idea was better – send him a box of candy and bug the chocolate creams.

PURKEY: Keep looking.

MAX (*eye on the finder*): Don't come unglued. We're okay.

54   INT. HARRY'S APARTMENT – DAY

Willie turns away from the radiator.

WILLIE: I think you'd better start for the airport, Boom Boom.

BOOM BOOM: Okay, coach.

HARRY: He's got an hour and a half.

WILLIE (*crosses to attaché case, opens it*): There's a lot of traffic. And those planes – you never know – they're late, they're early –

BOOM BOOM (*putting on his coat; to Harry*): Say, what do I call her – Mrs. Hinkle or Miss or

what?

HARRY (*a little grin*): Try Mrs.

BOOM BOOM: You got it.

He exits. Willie has taken some legal papers out of his attaché case, and with his back to the window, is scribbling something on the top page.

HARRY (*a sigh of relief, now that they are alone*): Boy, this brace is murder. If I don't get out of this chair, gangrene is going to set in.

He leans forward as if he were about to get up. But he is intercepted by Willie, who has come up quickly, and shoves the legal papers at him.

WILLIE: Look at this deposition!

HARRY: What do I know?

WILLIE (*firmly*): It's very important! Especially the footnote!

Harry glances down at the papers. At the bottom of the typed deposition, Willie has written in capital letters:

CAREFUL! WE ARE NOT ALONE!

WILLIE: Isn't that interesting?

Harry glances around the room, puzzled.

HARRY: I don't get it.

WILLIE: Take my word for it. A case like this is full of pitfalls. You can't just go skipping blithely through the wood like Little Riding Hood – there are wolves behind every tree – and you got to watch for grandma – because she's got *big eyes* and *big ears*.

HARRY: Oh?

55   INT. DETECTIVES' ROOM – DAY

Max, smoking a Tiparillo, is on the camera, Purkey is listening on the headset.

PURKEY (*to himself*): And big teeth! (*Max looks up*) He forgot the teeth.

MAX: He what?

PURKEY: I hate a guy who tells a story and louses up the punch-line.

56   INT. HARRY'S APARTMENT – DAY

Willie takes the legal papers from Harry, puts them back in the attaché case.

WILLIE: So the moral of the story is: – Better Red Riding Hood than *Dead* Riding Hood. You read me?

HARRY: Not really.

Willie, despairing, wanders off toward the bathroom.

WILLIE: Tell me – that whirlpool gadget Dr. Krugman prescribed –

HARRY: The Jacuzzi?

WILLIE: Yeah. Does it help you any?

HARRY: I suppose. Tones up the muscles or something.

Willie, in the bathroom now, looks down at the

Jacuzzi, standing in the empty tub.

WILLIE: Just exactly how does it work?

HARRY (*from living room*): Well, first you got to run some water in the tub.

WILLIE: All right.

He turns the water on full force. Then he peers at the bathroom radiator. Sure enough, there is another mike stashed there.

WILLIE (*to Harry*): How do you turn on this Jacuzzi thing?

HARRY (*in living room*): You just plug it in the wall.

WILLIE (*from bathroom*): You better come in and

show me.

Harry starts to wheel himself toward the bathroom.

57 INT. DETECTIVES' ROOM – DAY
Purkey is listening on the earphones. Max, his eye on the finder, changes the focus on the camera.

58 EXT. APARTMENT HOUSE – SECOND STORY WINDOWS – DAY
Through the finder Harry is seen as he wheels himself from the living room, across the bedroom, and into the bathroom.

59 INT. BATHROOM – DAY
The moment Harry is inside, Willie shuts the door.

HARRY: Would you mind telling me – ?

Willie clamps a hand across Harry's mouth, pulls out the hidden mike from the radiator, shows it to him. Harry watches wide-eyed as Willie hangs the mike over the top of the Jacuzzi. He now plugs the cord into the wall. The roar of the Jacuzzi in the half-filled tub echoes through the tiled bathroom.

60 INT. DETECTIVES' ROOM – DAY
Purkey almost leaps out of his skin as the sound hits him. He pulls the earphones away from his head. The Jacuzzi noise continues unabated.

61 INT. BATHROOM – DAY
The Jacuzzi is roaring away, right into the mike.

WILLIE: Okay – you can talk now.

HARRY: What the hell is going on here?

WILLIE: The whole place is bugged. And they're shooting from across the street.

HARRY (*up on his feet*): Shooting?

WILLIE: The detectives. With a camera.

HARRY (*pacing*): Well, who needs *that*? Get rid of them.

WILLIE: Not so fast.

HARRY: Pull down the shades and rip out the mikes. We're not going to put up with this.

WILLIE: Yes we are.

HARRY: What do you mean, we are?

WILLIE: Look, Harry – *we* know we're bugged – but *they* don't know we know. Don't you see the possibilities?

HARRY: No.

WILLIE: Anything we want to feed into those mikes, they'll swallow.

HARRY: Like what?

WILLIE (*sprawling in wheel-chair*): The only way to speed up the action is to goose them a little. It may take a year for this case to come to trial. You want to be stuck in this chair that long?

HARRY: A *year*?

WILLIE: Well, worry not – because I've got a scheme. And when we spring it on them, they're going to settle right away – and for big money.

HARRY: To hell with the big money. Give it to charity.

WILLIE: How did you guess?

HARRY: Huh?

WILLIE: That's the scheme.

FADE.

10. The Return of Tinker Bell

62 CLEVELAND AIRPORT – DAY
A United Airlines jet swoops down from the gray skies and comes in for a landing.

DISSOLVE:

63 BAGGAGE AREA – DAY
Passengers are lined up along the automatic conveyor, which is spewing out their luggage. Standing to one side, scanning the passengers, is Boom Boom. He spots Sandy. She is wearing a suit, a scarf over her head, and is carrying a coat.

As she is about to pick up her baggage – a suitcase and a makeup case – Boom Boom steps up.

BOOM BOOM: Mrs. Hinkle?

SANDY: Yes?

BOOM BOOM: Let me take those. (*reaches for the bags*) Mr. Gingrich sent me to pick you up.

SANDY: Oh? Has he got a chauffeur now?

BOOM BOOM: No – it's just that he's busy – with the lawsuit. (*leading her toward exit*) I'm a friend of Harry's.

SANDY: How is Harry?

BOOM BOOM: Much better. Now that he knows you're coming.

SANDY: And how's the lawsuit?

BOOM BOOM: Looks good. Mr. Gingrich thinks we can't lose.

SANDY: Oh, really?

BOOM BOOM: I'm going to testify for Harry myself. I'm a witness.

SANDY: You were there?

BOOM BOOM: Oh, yeah. Right where it happened. Actually, I'm the guy that hit him.

She throws him a look.

DISSOLVE:

64 INT. BOOM BOOM'S CADILLAC – DAY

Boom Boom is driving, Sandy is in the seat beside him.

BOOM BOOM: It's got me all shook up – I keep running that play over and over in my mind. I saw him standing there – I could've stepped out of bounds – I could've cut back and reversed my field – but I didn't. And all for a lousy extra five yards.

SANDY (*lighting a cigarette*): I wouln't brood about it. I mean, everybody tries for that extra five yards – and sometimes, people get in our way.

BOOM BOOM (*a sidelong glance, then –*): Harry played me your record. You sing good.

SANDY: I sing *damn* good, if you must know.

164

But I started off wrong – working with a cheap band in some crummy cellar. To make it these days, you need exposure.

BOOM BOOM: You need what?

SANDY: A showcase – like the Copa or the Persian Room. And for that you need a knockout wardrobe, and arrangements, and special material and a vocal coach and a publicity man – and for *that* you need money. So unless you've got like twenty thousand bucks, forget it.

BOOM BOOM: Maybe it's all for the best. Because – now that you're here, maybe you'll decide to stay.

SANDY (*a touch of sarcasm*): Sure. And go back to doing those linoleum commercials.

BOOM BOOM: I was talking about going back to Harry. (*no reaction from Sandy*) You know – you and I – we both hurt him. Except I can't do anything about it. But it's not too late for you to square things.

SANDY: We'll see what happens.

She removes her scarf, fishes some hair-pins out of her handbag, starts putting her hair up.

BOOM BOOM: When you travel with a football team, you live with a lot of guys. But Harry's something else again.

SANDY: You don't have to sell me.

BOOM BOOM: I wish you could have seen him this morning when your telegram came. (*Sandy continues putting her hair up*) All Mr. Gingrich talks about is the money – but all Harry talks about is you.

SANDY: That's just like him – sweet, impractical Harry. If he had his way, nobody would get anything out of this.

Boom Boom gives her another sidelong glance – a much longer one this time.

65 INT. HARRY'S APARTMENT – DAY

Harry, alone now, sits in the wheel-chair by the bay window, peering down the street, waiting expectantly for Sandy. He is wearing a cardigan over his corset, and has a blanket wrapped around his legs. After a moment, he becomes aware that the fingers of his left hand are drumming nervously on the arm-rest of the chair. He stops drumming, studies his hand. Then wheels himself to the television set. Among the other objects on it is a combination pipe-rack and tobacco jar. He lifts the lid off the jar, reaches into the tobacco, fishes out a wedding ring. He blows a few crumbs of tobacco from the ring, slips it on the third finger of his left hand. He closes the jar, wheels himself back to the window, looks out again. Suddenly his eyes light up, and he leans forward eagerly.

66 EAST 20th STREET – FROM
    HARRY'S POINT OF VIEW
The white Cadillac is just drawing up in front of the house. Boom Boom gets out, comes around the car, opens the other door, helps Sandy out. Her hair is all pinned up now, in an upswept style.

67 INT. DETECTIVES' ROOM – DAY
Purkey, earphones off, is threading a fresh tape into the recorder. Max, his eye glued to the camera, pans down toward the street.
MAX: Hey, get a load of that broad.
PURKEY: Keep your mind on business.
MAX: This *is* business. It's the wife. (*Purkey goes to the camera, looks through the finder*) I'd sure hate to be stuck in a wheel-chair with *her* around.

68 EAST 20th STREET – THROUGH
    FINDER
Boom Boom has taken the bags out of the car, and is following Sandy across the sidewalk into the apartment house.

69 INT. DETECTIVES' ROOM – DAY
Purkey turns to Max.
PURKEY: You got enough film in the camera?
MAX: Sure. Why?

PURKEY: Because if we're lucky, this may turn out to be our Swedish masseuse.
He clamps the earphones over his head, switches on the tape recorder.

70 INT. HARRY'S APARTMENT – DAY
Harry turns the wheel-chair away from the window, faces the door expectantly. He glances at the wedding ring on his finger, decides he may be overdoing it a little. He removes the ring, slips it into the pocket of his cardigan, just as a key is heard turning in the lock. Boom Boom opens the door for Sandy, follows her in with the bags. Sandy stops, looks off toward the bedroom.
HARRY: Hi, Sandy. (*she turns and sees him*) Have a good flight?
SANDY: Harry –
She rushes across the room, kneels beside him, embraces him.
HARRY: If I were a gentleman, I'd get up.
SANDY (*tears in her eyes*): Darling, darling – (*she kisses him, then steps back*) Let me look at you.
Harry fold his hands in his lap.
HARRY: What do I remind you of?
SANDY: I don't know. (*Harry starts whistling*) I still don't know.
HARRY: All right – one more clue.
He wheels himself over to the couch, stops right under the reproduction of Whistler's Mother. The similarity between his pose and hers is now obvious.
SANDY: Whistler's Mother! (*to Boom Boom*) Isn't he too much?
Harry takes her hand, draws her closer.
HARRY: Hey! What happened? You got green eyes.
SANDY: It's the contact lenses. They make them in all colors now.
HARRY: But you're still wearing your hair the way I like it.
SANDY: Oh, I've never changed.
Boom Boom takes this.

BOOM BOOM (*indicating bags*): Where do you want these? In the bedroom?

SANDY: Well, I certainly don't want them in the kitchen.

HARRY (*happily*): You heard the lady.

Boom Boom carries the bags into the bedroom. Sandy starts to take her coat off.

HARRY: How long can you stay?

SANDY: Well, it depends – the band is opening at some joint in Atlantic City – but I said I had to go to Cleveland to see a sick relative.

HARRY: That's close enough. I am sick – and I am a relative – at least I used to be.

Sandy has now seated herself on the ugly brown velveteen couch, and is taking her shoes off.

SANDY: Harry, promise me something. As soon as you get a little money, have this couch recovered.

HARRY: Don't worry. According to Willie, I can have it re-upholstered in hundred dollar bills. I may even get a new apartment – I already have a Mustang – Willie is breaking it in for me.

SANDY: Who cares? The important thing is to get you well again.

Boom Boom, who has reappeared in the archway from the bedroom, throws a contemptuous look in

her direction.

BOOM BOOM: I better start on that dinner.

HARRY: Thank you, Boom Boom.

Boom Boom goes through the swinging door into the kitchen.

SANDY (*drily*): Cooks, too. He's quite a treasure.

HARRY: I don't know what I would've done without him.

SANDY (*rises, crosses to window*): Harry – what do the doctors say?

HARRY: They're just guessing. It's a compressed vertebra – and some nerve damage – it all connects up.

SANDY (*frowning slightly*): Compressed vertebra?

HARRY: But I may fool them all. I may be back on my feet sooner than anyone expects – (*his eyes fall on the radiator, and he shifts gears abruptly*) On the other hand, you never know – sometimes these things drag on and on.

SANDY (*moving off*): Too bad it's a phony.

HARRY (*reacting*): What is?

SANDY: The fireplace. (*stops in front of it*) It would be nice to have a fire now.

HARRY: Remember when we used to put a red light bulb behind the logs – (*indicating throw rug*) – and pretend this was a bearskin rug?

SANDY (*smiling*): And right in front of Whistler's Mother.

HARRY: Shameless!

Sandy takes a flower from the vase, threads it through one of the perforations in Harry's corset.

SANDY: I'd better unpack.

She kisses him lightly on the cheek, goes into the bedroom. Harry looks after her for a moment, then wheels himself gaily toward the kitchen.

71   INT. KITCHEN – DAY

Boom Boom is unloading groceries from a couple of bags on the sink when Harry appears through the swinging door in his wheel chair.

HARRY: With the chicken paprika, I think we should have some white wine.

BOOM BOOM: I didn't get any.

HARRY: Look in the wine cellar – (*indicating cupboard*) – second shelf, behind the cereal – I hide it from the cleaning woman.

Boom Boom opens the cupboard door, removes the cereal boxes. There are a couple of bottles of domestic wine, half a bottle of vodka, three-quarters of a bottle of bourbon.

BOOM BOOM: I'll put it on ice.

HARRY: What do you think of Sandy? (*Boom Boom turns back toward sink*) I guess it's not fair to ask you – because you just met her. Not

167

that I think she's perfect – but then they're all a little unpredictable – and she may not be a raving beauty – but then I'm no Mastroianni, either. It's just that sometimes two people drift apart, but they have to get together again – because they're cut out for each other – like pieces of a jigsaw puzzle – they belong. You know what I'm trying to say?

BOOM BOOM: Yeah.

HARRY: I knew you'd agree with me.

He wheels himself happily out into the living room. Boom Boom looks after him, then reaches for a glass and the bourbon bottle, pours himself a shot, downs it.   FADE.

11. The Longest Night

72 INT. DETECTIVES' ROOM – NIGHT

The overhead light is on. Purkey, earphones around his neck is sitting on the bed, clipping his nails. Max is peering eagerly through the camera.

MAX: Oh boy, oh boy! Look at this!

PURKEY: What?

MAX: I think I'm going to go out of my mind! I can't watch it any more!

PURKEY (*leaning forward*): What?

MAX: Apricot dumplings!

PURKEY (*relaxing*): Oh.

MAX: On top of chicken paprika, red cabbage, buttered noodles – and that dame, she hasn't touched *any* of it. Just yak, yak, yak . . . (*pantomimes with his hand*)

73 INT. HARRY'S APARTMENT – NIGHT

There is a card table in the middle of the living room, covered with a tablecloth, and on it are dessert plates, wine glasses, and the remains of the bottle of wine. A single candle provides the only

illumination, but light comes from the kitchen and from a lamp on the night table in the bedroom. Sandy, wearing a cocktail dress, is sitting across the table from Harry, in his wheel-chair. She is smoking, and as Max so gracefully put it, yakking.*

SANDY: I knew it two weeks after I left you – what a terrible mistake I'd made. You have no idea how many times I wanted to pick up that phone and call you – but I was afraid – I thought you'd just hang up on me. Then when I heard about your accident, I didn't stop to think – I just called.

During this she has stubbed out her cigarette, picked up another one. Harry lights it for her.

HARRY: I'm glad you did. At least *something* good came out of it.

He pours the last of the wine into their glasses.

SANDY: The day I got the divorce papers, I was working in some club on Long Island, and I couldn't go on. I went to the ladies' room and was sick.

HARRY: You know what *I* did? I went down to Lake Erie, to throw my wedding ring away.

SANDY: I don't blame you. (*rises*) Let me show you something. (*goes into the bedroom, picks up her handbag*) You won't believe this, because you always said I wasn't the sentimental type – (*rummaging around inside bag*) Where is it?

She spills the contents of the bag out on the near bed – compact, lipsticks, brush, comb, hairpins, coins, keys, Kleenex, etc.

HARRY: What are you looking for?

He wheels himself up to the bed, where Sandy is searching through the mess.

HARRY: The junk you women carry around – it's like the inside of a claw machine.

SANDY: Here! (*she holds up a wedding ring*) I couldn't bear to throw it away.

HARRY (*after a beat; touched*): Well, now that you brought it up – neither could I.

He fishes his ring out of the pocket of his cardigan, holds it up. Their eyes meet and remain locked.

The kitchen door swings open and Boom Boom comes out with a pot of coffee and some demitasse cups on a tray.

BOOM BOOM: Where would you like your coffee?

HARRY (*snapping out of it*): Coffee? We'll have it in the library. (*to Sandy*) Or would you prefer the East Wing terrace?

SANDY (*smiling*): It's too cold for the terrace.

HARRY: The library it is. (*to Boom Boom*) And bring a third cup – join us.

BOOM BOOM: No, thanks. I don't want to butt into a family reunion.

He sets the tray down on the table, picks up the dessert dishes, exits into the kitchen. Sandy looks after him.

SANDY: I don't think he approves of me.

HARRY: Nonsense. You should have heard the way he was talking about you in the kitchen.

SANDY: Harry, now that I'm here – do you really need him any more?

HARRY: It's not that I need *him* – but he needs *me*. It makes him feel better to help me out.

SANDY: I thought that was going to be *my* job. You never considered me much of a wife – don't deny it – I guess I was kind of silly and

useless – but I want another chance now – maybe I've grown up a little.

HARRY (*after a moment*): You'd better pour the coffee. (*turns the wheel-chair, heads for the kitchen*) One lump – remember?

74   INT. KITCHEN – NIGHT

Boom Boom is at the sink, rinsing the dishes, when the door swings open and Harry wheels himself in.

HARRY: Never mind the dishes, Boom Boom. Leave them.

BOOM BOOM: Okay. They're all rinsed. (*dries his hands on a towel*) I'll finish up in the morning, when I come to fix your breakfast.

HARRY (*uncomfortable*): You don't have to bother.

Boom Boom picks up his jacket, puts it on.

BOOM BOOM: No bother. It's on the way to the practice field.

HARRY: Look, Boom Boom, I don't want to turn you into a housekeeper. You've got your own job to worry about. And now that Sandy is here – you know how it is –

BOOM BOOM (*nodding*): I know how it is.

He holds the door open for Harry, who is rather relieved that it all went so easily.

75   INT. HARRY'S APARTMENT – NIGHT

Sandy is at the table, having her coffee. Harry wheels himself out of the kitchen, followed by Boom Boom, who takes his coat off the peg.

BOOM BOOM: Mrs. Hinkle – that walker – he should practice with it every day. He's up to twenty steps now – he should try twenty-four tomorrow.

SANDY: Twenty-four? All right.

BOOM BOOM: And that whirlpool bath – he should take one twice a day. And if the batteries start to run down on the wheel-chair –

SANDY: I'll figure it out.

HARRY (*to Boom Boom*): You'll still come around
170

and see me, won't you?

BOOM BOOM (*big smile*): Sure, buddy. (*opens the door*) Good night.

HARRY: Good night.

Boom Boom exits.

SANDY: I didn't want to say anything in front of him, but that chicken dish we had –

HARRY: It's Hungarian.

SANDY: Well, it wasn't very good. *I've* learned to cook now.

HARRY: Really?

SANDY: I'll make you a meatloaf tomorrow. (*rises, turns her back to him*) Unzip me, please.

Harry pulls the zipper down.

HARRY: You've put on a little weight.

Sandy moves into the bedroom, steps out of her dress.

SANDY: Seven pounds. That's how good a cook I am. (*takes a nightgown out of the closet*) If you need any help with your corset –

HARRY: I can manage.

Sandy goes into the bathroom, closes the door. Harry watches her from his wheel-chair – after a year away from her, this is more than he can take. He sips his coffee, but his mind is on other things. Abruptly, he swings himself around to the phonograph, switches it on. The record on the turntable is mood music – lush and romantic. Then he heads for the open door of the kitchen, reaches inside, turns off the kitchen light. On the way back he locks the hall door, circles the table, picks up the candle. As he wheels himself into the bedroom, clearly ready to throw all caution to the winds, the phone rings in the living room. Harry stops, glances over his shoulder with annoyance. The bathroom door opens and Sandy comes out, in her nightgown.

SANDY: The phone, darling. Aren't you going to answer it?

Harry stares at her wordlessly. She moves past him into the living room, picks up the phone.

SANDY: Hello? . . . Yes? . . . I'm just fine.

76 INT. WILLIE'S APARTMENT –
NIGHT

Willie is sitting at the phone in the hallway. Through an arch beyond him Charlotte can be seen in the dining room, clearing the dinner dishes off the table.

WILLIE: Well, welcome to Cleveland. Certainly nice to have you back with the organization. How's our boy?

Jeffrey and Ginger appear from around a bend in the hallway, on their skateboards, go rumbling past him.

WILLIE: Why don't you kids go play on the freeway? *(into phone)* I said – how's our boy?

77 INT. HARRY'S APARTMENT –
NIGHT

SANDY *(into phone)*: He's wonderful – everything's wonderful – like old times. *(Harry wheels himself toward phone)* We just had dinner, and we're about to go to bed.

78 INT. WILLIE'S APARTMENT –
NIGHT

WILLIE *(into phone)*: You are. Let me talk to him. *(scowls thoughtfully while he waits)* Look, Harry, if I were you I'd forget it . . . Oh, come on – I know what's going through your mind. But this is not the time – or the place.

79 INT. HARRY'S APARTMENT –
NIGHT

Harry, in his wheel-chair, is at the phone. Sandy is moving off toward the bedroom.

HARRY: What are you, my marriage counsellor? If I want any advice, I'll write to Dear Abby.

80 INT. WILLIE'S APARTMENT –
NIGHT

WILLIE *(into phone)*: Okay, Harry, it's your neck . . . But if you're going to do something foolish, just remember to show your good

171

profile – because you're on Candid Camera!

He bangs the receiver down. Jeffrey and Ginger come skating past. At the same time, Charlotte starts out of the dining room into the kitchen with a load of dishes. She disappears through the swinging door just as the kids disappear around a bend in the hallway. A beat – then there is a shouted warning from Charlotte, and a tremendous crash of china and glassware. Willie continues to sit beside the phone, paying no attention.

81   INT. HARRY'S APARTMENT –
       NIGHT

Harry has hung up, but is still staring at the phone. Then he glances toward the bedroom, where Sandy is just getting into bed. Now comes a long look toward the window and the detectives across the street.

SANDY (*from bedroom*): Harry – are you all right?

HARRY (*miserably*): I'm fine.

Making his decision, he wheels himself over to the bookcase, takes out a book. It is THE CARPETBAGGERS, hard-cover. He snuffs out the candle, and armed with the book, heads grimly into the bedroom. FADE.

12. The Other Blonde

82   INT. BOOM BOOM'S BOWLING
       ALLEY – NIGHT

A glass partition separates the cocktail lounge from the lanes, and both parts of the establishment are jumping. The bartenders and waiters wear shirts with BOOM BOOM'S BOWLING lettered on their backs.

Boom Boom is sitting at the bar, downing a double shot of bourbon. He sets the glass down, beckons to one of the bartenders. The man is about fifty, and looks like a former boxer, which is exactly what he is – for this is Boom Boom's

172

father, who runs the place for him.

BOOM BOOM: I'll have one more of these.

MR. JACKSON (*shaking his head*): Sorry.

BOOM BOOM: What do you mean, sorry?

MR. JACKSON: The management reserves the right to refuse service to anyone.

BOOM BOOM: I own this joint.

MR. JACKSON: But you appointed me the management, and I say no.

BOOM BOOM: Now cut that out, Pop. I need it.

MR. JACKSON: If you want to drown yourself, use water. This won't do it. I know – I tried it once myself.

He moves off along the bar.

Sitting in a booth against the wall, watching this scene with interest, is a sultry colored girl with blonde upswept hair. Her name is ELVIRA, and there are three husky men in the booth with her. She picks up a shot glass from in front of one of her companions, rises, crosses to the bar, slides the drink towards Boom Boom. He looks up at her.

BOOM BOOM: What's that?

ELVIRA: Bourbon. (*she sits on the stool beside him*) Haven't seen you around for a long time. (*Boom Boom stares at her blankly*) It's me – Elvira. I bleached my hair. (*fluffs it up with one hand*) You like it?

BOOM BOOM (*flat*): It's gorgeous.

ELVIRA: You know what they say – blondes have more fun.

BOOM BOOM: Yeah. Because there's always some sucker to pay for it. (*shoves the drink back toward her*) Beat it.

ELVIRA: What did I do?

BOOM BOOM: I said beat it.

The man whose drink Elvira appropriated rises from the booth, saunters up to the bar, a cigarette dangling from his lips.

MAN: He bothering you, honey?

BOOM BOOM: Why don't you take honey home and dip her head in a pot of ink?

MAN (*to Elvira*): Real tough cat, ain't he?

Except on that football field. He didn't look so tough against the Giants last Sunday.

With a deliberate gesture, Boom Boom plucks the cigarette out of the man's mouth, tosses it away, then pushes him in the face. Elvira screams. The man goes staggering back toward the booth, upsets the table. His two companions jump up, bear down on Boom Boom. Boom Boom comes off his stool swinging. As a mêlée develops, Elvira's escort joins the other two in ganging up on Boom Boom.

Out of the kitchen comes Mr. Jackson.

MR. JACKSON: All right, break it up!

He wades in, becomes involved in the fight. As the battle reaches a climax, the SOUND of an approaching police siren is HEARD.

FADE.

13. The Indian Givers

83   INT. DETECTIVES' ROOM – DAY

A bleary-eyed Max is sitting beside the camera, earphones on, while Purkey is stretched out on the bed, covered with his coat, catching a little shut-eye. Max stretches, cracks his knuckles. Purkey sits up as though he's been shot.

PURKEY: Anything happen across the street?

MAX: I'll say. You missed all the action. She gave him a rubdown, he gave *her* a rubdown –

PURKEY (*on his feet; excitedly*): Did you get it on film?

MAX (*rising*): Cool it! Nothing happened. He fell asleep in the wheel-chair, and she stayed up reading and smoking a lot. (*hands over earphones*) It's your turn to drive. Don't wake me till we get to Albuquerque.

He flops down on the bed. Purkey puts on the earphones, seats himself beside the camera.

84   INT. HARRY'S APARTMENT – DAY

Harry, dressed the way he was the night before,

is sitting in his wheel-chair, speaking into the phone. Sandy, wearing a robe over her night-gown, is vacuuming the rug in the bedroom.

HARRY: Oh, I'm doing fine. . . . Sure I miss you. But Sandy's here, and she's taking good care of me. (*he pulls the receiver away from his ear, and we hear Mother Hinkle sobbing at the other end*) Please don't cry, mother. . . . Believe me, she's changed – right now she's vacuuming the rug – and tonight she's making a meatloaf. (*pulls the receiver away from his ear; more sobs from Mother Hinkle*) Mother, please stop crying. . . . How's the weather in Florida?

Again her sobbing forces him to remove the receiver from his ear. The doorbell rings. Sandy switches the vacuum cleaner off, opens the door. It's Willie – chesterfield, Homburg and attaché case.

WILLIE: Hi, Sandy. (*kisses her on the cheek*) Good morning, Harry (*hears the crying over the phone, takes the receiver from Harry*) Shut up, mother!

HARRY (*grabbing the phone back*): Don't mind him. Now you go back to your canasta game – I'll call you over the weekend.

He hangs up.

WILLIE (*to Sandy*): You look very yummy for this early in the morning.

SANDY: I *feel* yummy.

WILLIE (*to Harry, suspiciously*): Everything under control?

HARRY (*sourly*): Everything.

Willie opens the attaché case, takes out some legal forms.

WILLIE: I've got the incorporation papers here. Sign all seven copies.

He hands the forms and a pen to Harry.

SANDY: What are you incorporating?

WILLIE (*for the benefit of the mike in the radiator*): The Harry Hinkle Foundation. (*to Harry*) Didn't you tell her?

HARRY: I thought it was supposed to be a surprise.

SANDY: I don't like surprises. What's this all about?

WILLIE: Oh, you're going to be proud of him when you hear this . . .

Harry has started signing the papers. As Willie explains the scheme to Sandy, he tosses the key phrases in the direction of the mike.

WILLIE: Next Saturday, there's going to be a night game against Washington . . . and between the halves, they're planning a tribute to Harry. The lights are going to go out, and everybody will be asked to light a match and say a silent prayer for Harry's recovery. Can't you just see it – 83,000 matches flickering in that dark stadium? Then the spotlight will pick up Harry – he'll wheel himself up to the microphone – and make the announcement.

SANDY: What announcement?

WILLIE: That all the money he gets from the insurance company, over and above his actual

medical expenses, is going to go into the Harry Hinkle Foundation to Help the Handicapped.

SANDY (*frowning*): I'm not sure I understand.

WILLIE: We don't want anybody to think we're suing just to line our own pockets. Maybe we're not the Rockefeller Institute or the Ford Foundation – but in our own small way we can hold out a hand to the less fortunate – give them a little hope – a leg to stand on.

85 INT. DETECTIVES' ROOM – DAY

Purkey is listening with interest, and growing concern. Finally he removes the earphones, shakes Max, who is flaked out on the bed.

PURKEY: Wake up!

MAX: What is it?

PURKEY: We're in Albuquerque.

MAX: Huh?

PURKEY: Something important just came up. I want to take this tape down to Mr. O'Brien.

He hands the earphones to Max, who drags himself wearily out of bed and over to the camera.

MAX: I should have listened to my mother and become a bookie.

Purkey has removed the spool of tape from the machine, puts it in a box, hurries out.

86 INT. HARRY'S APARTMENT – DAY

Harry finishes signing the last of the papers, hands them to Willie.

HARRY (*pointing*): Shouldn't Handicapped have two p's?

WILLIE: Oh, I typed it myself – trying to save a little money – after all, it's a non-profit organization.

He puts the paper back in the attaché case. Sandy, meanwhile, is lost in thought.

HARRY (*to Sandy*): You're not disappointed, are you?

SANDY: About what?

HARRY: Re-upholstering the couch.

SANDY: What are you talking about? I think it's a wonderful thing you're doing. (*kisses him*

175

on the cheek) And I'm *very* proud of you.

WILLIE: Well, I'd better be getting back to the office. I'm expecting an important phone call. (*crosses to door, opens it*) 83,000 matches. I hope it doesn't rain.

He exits.

SANDY (*suddenly*): Oh, Willie – (*to Harry*) Be right back.

She hurries after Willie.

Willie has started down the steps as Sandy comes out of the apartment, shutting the door behind her.

SANDY: Hey, Santa Claus – (*Willie stops, turns*) Can I ask you a question?

WILLIE: Sure, little girl. Would you like to sit on my lap?

SANDY: What's all this about helping the handicapped? What's the gag?

WILLIE (*innocently*): Gag?

SANDY: Oh, come off it, Willie. Why would you go to the trouble of trumping up a case and then give the money away?

WILLIE: Who says it's trumped up?

SANDY: *I* do. You think I'm stupid?

WILLIE: Five specialists examined him. You think *they're* stupid?

SANDY: Compressed vertebra! Harry has had that since he was a kid. So don't snow me. I know it's a fraud.

WILLIE (*wincing*): I wish you wouldn't use words like that.

SANDY: And so is the Foundation.

WILLIE: Let's just say it's a legal maneuver – to put the squeeze on the insurance company. They can go to court and fight *me* – but they wouldn't dare fight an organized charity.

SANDY (*glancing back toward apartment*): If anybody had told me that Harry would get involved in something like this . . .

WILLIE: It wasn't easy. And he may still blow it. The whole place is wired for sound – and

there are detectives watching from across the street.

SANDY: I get the picture.

WILLIE: I hope *they* don't. So if you could keep him in line, I'd appreciate it very much.

SANDY: *How* much?

WILLIE: Worry not. There'll be enough for everybody.

SANDY: I'll do what I can.

WILLIE: That's a good kid. (*he pats her on the behind; she slaps his hand away*) Put on a little weight, haven't you? (*starts down the stairs*) I'd say about seven pounds.

Sandy turns back into the apartment.

Harry is sitting where we left him when Sandy comes in.

SANDY: Sorry. I just wanted some legal advice from Willie.

HARRY: About what?

SANDY: I was wondering – if you can annul a marriage – why can't you annul a divorce?

HARRY: Can you?

SANDY: You know Willie – if there's a loophole, he'll find it. (*picks up walker*) Time to practice with your walker. Twenty-four steps today.

She carries the walker towards Harry.

FADE.

14. The Gravy Train

On the desk is a tape recorder, replaying Willie's announcement that the insurance money is going into the Harry Hinkle Foundation to Help the Handicapped. Gathered around, listening incredulously, are O'Brien, Thompson and Kincaid. Standing to one side is Purkey, still in his overcoat, hat in hand. Finally O'Brien snaps the machine off angrily.

O'BRIEN: Are you sure that's the voice of Willie Gingrich?

PURKEY: Yeah. Recorded this morning.

THOMPSON: Whiplash Willie turning philanthropist. Do you believe that?

KINCAID: Not for a second.

O'BRIEN: Gentlemen, do you realize what this means?

THOMPSON: It's obviously some sort of cheap trick.

O'BRIEN: I wouldn't call it cheap. The minute a jury hears that the money is going to charity, they'll nail the insurance company for the maximum. A million dollars.

PURKEY: I still think Hinkle is an imposter.

O'BRIEN: You think!

PURKEY: I know I've let you down . . .

O'BRIEN: You certainly have. In technicolor!

PURKEY: I better be getting back to my post.
He backs out the door, putting his hat on.

O'BRIEN: Poor Purkey! Used to be the best private eye in Cleveland. (*to Kincaid*) Get Gingrich on the phone.

THOMPSON: What for?

O'BRIEN: We're in a good position to negotiate – because we know he's up to something – but he doesn't know we know.

KINCAID: You want to settle?

O'BRIEN: As quickly as we can.

THOMPSON: Settle a phony claim? What about our integrity?

O'BRIEN: Gentlemen, we're merely acting for the client. It's no longer a question of our integrity, it's a question of their money.
Kincaid picks up the phone.

90   INT. GINGRICH OFFICE – DAY
Willie is sitting at his desk, staring at the phone as though trying to hypnotize it into ringing. Finally it does ring. Willie grins, lets it ring a couple of more times, then picks up the receiver.
WILLIE: Hello? . . . Yes? . . . O'Brien, Thompson and *who*? . . . Oh, yes. You're those

lawyers in my building. What's on your mind, gentlemen? . . . You want to see me? Let me check my calendar –
Humming the overture to 'The Barber of Seville', he fishes out a dusty appointment book from the shambles on his desk, starts to leaf through the completely blank pages.
WILLIE: Well, I'm all jammed up tomorrow – nothing open Thursday – Friday is out of the question – maybe I can squeeze you in next Monday, between eleven and eleven-fifteen. . . . Today? I just don't see how I can do it. . . . Well, if you boys want to drop down here and

take your chances. . . . All rightie.

He hangs up smugly. Then he rises, glances around the office, decides to do a little light house-cleaning. He gathers up stacks of books, papers and other debris, piles them onto the already crowded desk. When the desk is loaded, he starts to pull down the roll-top to hide the mess. The tambour top reaches the level of the desk, continues to slide right out of its grooves, hits the floor. As Willie stares down at his feet, the door opens, revealing O'Brien, Thompson and Kincaid.

WILLIE: Come on in.

He picks up the loose roll-top, leans it against the wall, as the three lawyers file in, look around with distaste.

WILLIE: I'm sorry things are a little messy around here – you see, my secretary got married.

KINCAID: Oh, really?

WILLIE: Yeah. Ten years ago. To me. (*expansively*) Sit down, sit down.

He waves O'Brien toward a rickety chair, surrenders his own chair to Kincaid, upends a wastepaper basket to make a seat for Thompson.

WILLIE: Now what's your problem, gentlemen?

O'BRIEN: Well, Consolidated Insurance would like to wrap up the Hinkle case before the first of the year – simply as a matter of bookkeeping. Mind you, it's against our advice – but on their behalf, we're prepared to offer you ten thousand dollars.

WILLIE: Let me see – if you're offering ten thousand, that means you've been authorized to go to twenty-five. And if you're authorized to go to twenty-five, that means they're willing to go to fifty. So why don't we skip all the preliminaries, and start at fifty thousand.

THOMPSON: *Fifty thousand dollars?*

WILLIE: That's not acceptable.

The kettle on the hot-plate starts boiling. Willie moves toward it.

WILLIE: Would you gentlemen like to have some instant coffee?

KINCAID: We'd like to have an instant decision.

O'BRIEN: We *might* go as high as twenty-five thousand.

WILLIE: What's your hurry, gentlemen? We'll all have our day in court. I'm perfectly willing to leave the decision to a jury – twelve good men and true.

The three lawyers exchange worried glances.

O'BRIEN: Thirty-five thousand.

By now Willie has taken a jar of instant coffee and a cup from a shelf above the hot plate. Also stacked on the shelf are various other jars, cans, bottles, cracker boxes, etc.

WILLIE: Anybody care for some cocoa? Ovaltine? Sauerkraut juice? Delaware Punch?

O'BRIEN: Forty thousand.

WILLIE: Melba toast? Skinless and boneless sardines? Tootsie rolls? Low calorie yoghurt? (*digs something out*) How about a pepperoni pizza?

O'BRIEN: No, thanks. I'm on Metrecal.

WILLIE: Metrecal? Fresh out. (*opens medicine cabinet over wash-basin*) But I have Bufferin, Pepto-Bismol, mercurochrome –

O'BRIEN: Forty-*five* thousand.

WILLIE: You boys going to the game Saturday? It's Harry Hinkle Night. There's going to be a very interesting show between the halves.

Another exchange of looks between the three lawyers.

O'BRIEN: Fifty thousand. Take it or leave it.

Willie busies himself fixing the instant coffee.

WILLIE: Gentlemen, when this case started, I wrote down a figure on a piece of paper. I've got it right here. (*takes scrap of paper out of his pocket*) I will not settle for a cent less than that.

O'BRIEN: All right. Fifty-five thousand dollars.

WILLIE: Did you say fifty-*five* thousand?

The three lawyers nod eagerly. Willie unfolds the piece of paper.

WILLIE: That's not it.

He refolds it, puts it back in his pocket.

DISSOLVE TO:

91 INT. HARRY'S APARTMENT –
   NIGHT

*Harry and Sandy are watching the evening
newscast on television. Harry is in his wheel-
chair, Sandy is on the couch, doing her nails.
She has a wastepaper basket in front of her, and
resting on top of it is a small tray containing
polish, polish remover, cotton pads, file, orange
stick, etc.
On the TV screen, a news announcer is sitting at*
*a desk, speaking into a mike. Projected on the
wall behind him is an aerial view of flooded
homes.*

ANNOUNCER: . . . has been declared a disaster
area. Eleven persons are dead or missing, over
two hundred families have been evacuated from
their homes, and property damage is estimated
in the millions. . . . I'll be back with more news
after this word from our sponsor.

SANDY (*expectantly*): Here it comes.

*A commercial flashes on the screen – a girl in a
long chiffon dress, dancing between columns of
linoleum.*

GIRL (*singing*):
Cover your floors with Lindenbaum's Linoleum
It's better indoors with Lindenbaum's Lino-
leum
For the lowest price and the highest style
Do your house over in vinyl tile
And for gracious living come down to
Lindenbaum's
Come down to Lindenbaum's
Come down to Lindenbaum's . . .
*Over the last part of her dance is SUPERIM-
POSED: LINDENBAUM'S LINOLEUM,
9th and Plum; No Money Down, 18 Months to
Pay.*
During this, Sandy is eyeing the girl critically.
SANDY: I don't want to be bitchy – but where
did they dig *her* up?
HARRY: She sings a little flat, doesn't she?
SANDY: Flat? She's pitiful. . . . And how
about that long dress? She must have bad legs.
I used to do it in tights.
HARRY: You don't have to remind me. I was
on the camera.
*The commercial is over and the announcer
reappears on the screen.*
ANNOUNCER: On the local scene, the chances
of the Cleveland Browns to repeat as National
Football League champions suffered a blow
last night when one of their star performers ran
afoul of the law.
*A picture of Boom Boom, in uniform, flashes on
the wall behind him.*
Harry reacts, leans forward in his wheel-chair.
ANNOUNCER: Luther Boom Boom Jackson,
leading punt-returner in the League, was
released on bail today after being charged with
drunkenness, assault and battery and resisting
arrest. Art Modell, owner of the Browns,
announced this afternoon that Jackson has been
indefinitely suspended, pending a hearing to
determine further disciplinary action. (*Boom
Boom's picture fades out*) In other news from the
world of sports, Mickey Mantle said in

Oklahoma City today –
*By this time, Harry has wheeled himself up to
the set and snapped it off.*
SANDY: That's a shame.
HARRY (*grimly*): I knew it! I knew I shouldn't
let him out of my sight!
*He wheels himself around, heads for the phone.
Sandy, her hands held out zombie-like in front of
her, watches him worriedly as he starts to dial a
number.*
SANDY: Who are you calling?
Harry doesn't answer.

92   INT. GINGRICH OFFICE – EVENING

*They're still at it – Willie versus O'Brien,
Thompson and Kincaid. Willie is as cool as a
cucumber, but the three lawyers are somewhat the
worse for wear – coats off, ties askew, dead cigar
stubs in their mouths. Empty coffee cups and
other dishes are scattered around. O'Brien, who
has been in a huddle with his partners, finally
comes out of it.*
O'BRIEN: This is absolutely our final offer –
one hundred and twenty-five thousand dollars.
*Willie produces the folded scrap of paper from
his pocket, consults it.*
WILLIE: Wrong again.
*As he puts the paper away, the phone rings, and
he picks up the receiver.*
WILLIE: Hello? . . . What is it, kid?

93   INT. HARRY'S APARTMENT – EVENING

Harry, in his wheel-chair, is at the phone.
HARRY: Did you hear what happened to Boom
Boom? . . . Well, I'm sure he must need a
lawyer.

94   INT. GINGRICH OFFICE – EVENING

*Willie on the phone, the three lawyers slumping
in exhaustion.*

WILLIE: There are 4100 lawyers in Cleveland – and you have to pick on the one who's beating his brains out for you? There's nothing we can do for him anyway. . . . Come on, Harry – don't bother me – we got bigger fish to fry. (*hangs up, turns to the lawyers*) All right, gentlemen.

He picks up a judge's gavel, bangs it on the desk like an auctioneer's hammer.

WILLIE: Do I hear a hundred and fifty thousand?

95 INT. HARRY'S APARTMENT – EVENING

Harry turns slowly away from the phone, sits there brooding. Sandy rises from the couch, picks up the manicure tray, starts toward the bedroom.

SANDY: What did Willie say?

HARRY (*bitterly*): He can't be bothered. He's negotiating.

With sudden violence, he kicks the wastepaper basket across the room. Sandy quickly sets the tray down, throws a worried look toward the window.

SANDY: Harry – be careful!

HARRY: You want to know who got him into this mess? You want to know the whole story?

96 INT. DETECTIVES' ROOM – EVENING

Max is at the camera, Purkey is listening intently on the earphones.

97 INT. HARRY'S APARTMENT – EVENING

Sandy hurries toward Harry, keeping an eye on the window.

SANDY: Darling, don't get gray hair over it.

HARRY: I've been lying to you all along.

He leans forward in the wheel-chair, about to get up. Sandy puts her arm around him, restraining him, kneels beside him, runs her other hand across his temple.

SANDY: You do have a few gray hairs. Makes you look distinguished.

She kisses him on the cheek, and at the same time, puts a finger to his lips.

SANDY (*an intense whisper*): Don't move, don't say anything. Just think about you and me. If we're to start all over again, how can it hurt to have a little money? We're so close to it now – don't throw it away.

Realization is slowly dawning on Harry's face.

98 INT. DETECTIVES' ROOM – EVENING

Purkey is straining to hear the whispered conversation. He hits his earphone with the heel of his hand, then removes it, cleans his ear with his pinkie, listens again.

99 INT. HARRY'S APARTMENT – EVENING

Sandy, her cheek still pressed against Harry's, continues to whisper in his ear, Svengali-like.

SANDY: For once in your life, be practical – do the smart thing. I love you, Harry – but I don't want to love somebody dumb.

Harry is plainly torn. Sandy kisses him passionately – and after a moment, he responds.

FADE.

15. The Better Mousetrap

100 EXT. EAST 20th STREET – NIGHT

The Mustang drives up in front of the apartment house and out steps Willie, attaché case in hand, an expression of smug self-satisfaction on his face. He is about to enter the apartment house, stops. He turns and looks up toward the detectives'

hideout in the rooming house across the street.
WILLIE (*calling*): Hey, Purkey? You hear me?
Purkey?

101 EXT. WINDOW OF ROOMING HOUSE – NIGHT
There is a dim light coming through the shade, as is the telescopic lens of the camera.
WILLIE'S VOICE: I know you're up there.

102 INT. DETECTIVES' ROOM – NIGHT
Only the small lamp on the night-stand is burning. Max is at the camera, Purkey is sitting on the bed, the dictaphone in front of him, the earphones off.
WILLIE'S VOICE (*from the street*): You're not fooling anybody, you big tub of lard!
Purkey springs to his feet angrily.
MAX: How does he know we're – ?
Purkey clamps a hand across his mouth.

103 EXT. EAST 20th STREET – NIGHT
Willie is standing in front of the apartment house entrance, shouting up toward the detectives' window.
WILLIE: I got a message for you – from Gemini Control. You can start packing up – because the mission has been scrubbed! Repeat – the mission has been scrubbed! Over and out!
He chuckles, starts into the apartment house, gaily humming the overture to 'The Barber of Seville'.

104 INT. DETECTIVES' ROOM – NIGHT
Purkey still has his hand against Max's mouth. Max pushes it away.
MAX: Take that filthy glove out of my face. (*wipes his mouth*) You suppose he's telling the truth?
PURKEY: I wouldn't put *anything* past him.

182

He stoops low, sneaks past the window so as not to cast a shadow on the blind, picks up the phone.
PURKEY: Let me check it out with Mr. O'Brien.
He starts to dial.

105 INT. HARRY'S APARTMENT – EVENING
Harry is sitting in his wheel-chair, motionless, his back to the window. From the landing comes the sound of Willie's voice, humming the overture to 'The Barber of Seville'. Sandy emerges from the kitchen, carrying a coffee service on a tray, just as the doorbell rings. She sets the tray down on the end table, opens the door. Willie breezes in.
WILLIE: Am I early? I hate to be the first one at a party.
SANDY: What party?
Willie tosses his hat and the attaché case on the couch, starts to take off his coat.
WILLIE: I thought we were having a little celebration tonight.
SANDY (*catching on*): Willie – what happened?
WILLIE: This *is* the Hinkle apartment, isn't it?
SANDY: Come on – tell us.
Willie starts removing the coffee pot, cups, cream and sugar from the tray.
WILLIE: Whereas Harry Hinkle, hereinafter referred to as the plaintiff, has agreed to renounce all claims, past, present and future, against the Cleveland Browns, CBS and the Municipal Stadium, hereinafter referred to as the defendants – in consideration thereof . . .
He takes a check out of his pocket, slaps it on the tray, holds it out to Harry.
WILLIE: Like I promised you – on a silver platter.
Harry extends his hand – but points beyond the tray.
HARRY: Can I have my coffee, please?
Sandy snatches the check from the tray.
SANDY: Two hundred thousand dollars!
WILLIE: I could have held out for more. But old Mr. O'Brien – I took pity on him – I hate

to see a grown man cry.

SANDY (*still studying the check*): I may cry myself. Look at all those zeroes. (*throws her arms around Willie*) Willie, you're a genius!

She twirls him around the room, waving the check aloft. Willie, falling into the spirit of it, manipulates the tray like a tambourine.

WILLIE (*singing to the tune of the 'Barber of Seville' Overture*):

> I'm a genius
> Yes, I'm a genius
> I'm a genuine, bona fide genius
> An ever-loving, card-carrying genius . . .

Harry honks his horn sharply.

HARRY: I'd *still* like my coffee.

WILLIE: Coffee? At a time like this? (*to Sandy*) You wouldn't have any champagne on ice?

SANDY: We don't even have ice. The refrigerator broke down. (*hands check back to Willie*) I'll see what I can find.

She exits into the kitchen. Willie eyes his brooding brother-in-law.

WILLIE: Come on, Harry – cheer up. You just got the biggest cash award ever made in a personal injury case in the State of Ohio – and you're acting like a loser.

HARRY: Well, what do you want me to do? Put a lampshade on my head? Turn cartwheels?

WILLIE: Not yet. You're still convalescing. But in a few weeks we'll have you up on crutches – then after a while we'll get you a cane –

HARRY: Why are you so good to me?

WILLIE: So you'll be walking to the bank with a slight limp. Big deal.

106 INT. DETECTIVES' ROOM – NIGHT

Purkey is on the phone.

PURKEY: Okay, Mr. O'Brien – if that's the way you want it – you're the boss. (*slams the receiver down; to Max*) They settled!

MAX (*glancing at wrist-watch*): Good! I can wrap up and still get home in time to watch Batman.

He starts to dismantle the camera.

PURKEY: Don't touch that camera!

MAX: The case is over.

PURKEY: That's what you think – and that's what Gingrich thinks.

MAX: Why don't you give up already? He's too smart for you.

PURKEY: Maybe so. But Hinkle isn't. And I think I know how to break him down.

He crosses to the door, opens it.

MAX: Where are you going?

PURKEY: The big tub of lard is going to pay a little visit across the street. So stand by for action.

He exits. Max puts his eye to the camera finder.

107 INT. HARRY'S APARTMENT – EVENING

Sandy has returned to the room, and is filling three glasses from a liqueur bottle.

WILLIE (*to Harry*): Now that you got this kind of money, you'll have to be very careful. Because the world is full of chiselers and con men –

HARRY: I'll be careful.

WILLIE: But luckily, you got me. You may think I'm a great lawyer – but I'm ten times as good a business manager.

HARRY: I'll be *very* careful.

Sandy hands each of them a liqueur glass.

SANDY (*toasting*): Happy days.

WILLIE: What's this?

SANDY: Kahlua.

WILLIE: *Kahlua?*

SANDY: I thought we had some bourbon – (*to Harry*) – but your friend Boom Boom –

She and Willie down their drinks. Harry continues to hold the glass in his hand.

WILLIE: Now when it comes to investing, the big trick is diversification. You put a little

183

money in uranium stocks – a few oil wells in Montana – some real estate in downtown Phoenix –

SANDY: As long as you boys are diversifying – I want twenty thousand dollars to invest in me.

HARRY: In you?

SANDY: That's what it would cost to put an act together – if I'm to work the Persian Room.

WILLIE: You going back into the singing racket?

SANDY: You bet. And this time I'm going to do it right.

HARRY (*studying her*): For twenty thousand dollars you can put on a pretty good act.

SANDY: 'Everything's Coming Up Roses' – that's what I want to open with. Four guys carry me on in a big basket of flowers – I'm wearing a tight red sequin gown, and they're in tails – white tie, top hats and canes –

WILLIE: Socko, baby, socko.

HARRY (*drily*): Maybe I can be one of the four guys. I'll bring my own cane.

The doorbell rings.

WILLIE: Well, the party's beginning to build. (*he opens the door, revealing Purkey*) I take it back.

PURKEY: Can I come in for a minute?

WILLIE: You mean through the door? I thought you only came in through the window – or through the heating system.

PURKEY: If you don't mind – now that it's all over – I'd like to take out my equipment.

WILLIE: Help yourself.

Purkey nods to Harry and Sandy, heads toward the bathroom.

WILLIE: You know something, Purkey – we're going to miss you around here. Because you were a real good neighbor – quiet, unobtrusive, and yet always keeping a watchful eye on us. *In the bathroom, Purkey takes out a pair of pliers, cuts the wire of the microphone in the radiator.*

PURKEY: I was just doing my job. Nothing

184

personal.

WILLIE: Of course not. But sometimes even the best bloodhound barks up the wrong tree.

Purkey has now returned to the bedroom. As he heads for the radiator, Willie reaches down, yanks the microphone out, hands it to him. Purkey smiles sourly, proceeds into the living room.

PURKEY (*as he passes Harry*): Any more news about Boom Boom Jackson?

HARRY: No.

PURKEY (*moving toward radiator*): Too bad what happened to him. But maybe it'll teach him a lesson. Our black brothers, they've been getting a little out of hand lately. Just too damn cocky – you know what I mean?

Harry grips the arms of the wheel-chair tightly. Willie senses the danger.

WILLIE (*to Purkey*): That's enough out of you.

PURKEY: Look, I'm all for equal. But what gets me is – I'm driving an old Chevvy. And when I see a coon riding around in a white Cadillac – *Harry leaps out of the wheel-chair, tossing his glass away.*

HARRY: You son of a –

On 'bitch' he socks Purkey in the jaw, and Purkey sits down heavily on the floor.

WILLIE: Harry! (*grabs him*)

Purkey tests his jaw, then grins up at Harry.

PURKEY: Thanks.

He scrambles to his feet, hurries to the window, throws it open.

PURKEY (*shouting across the street*): Max!

WILLIE (*to Harry*): You walked right into a trap, you idiot!

SANDY (*bitterly*): I'm the idiot. I should have tipped off the insurance company – *they* would have given me twenty thousand dollars.

Harry stares at her.

PURKEY (*leaning out the window*): Hey, Max!

The shade in the detectives' room goes up, and we see Max standing beside the camera.

PURKEY: Did you get it?

MAX (*shouting back*): I'm not sure. It's a little dark.

Willie sees a chance to salvage the situation.

WILLIE (*to Harry, in a sharp whisper*): Did you hear that? Get back in the chair.

He tries to force Harry into the wheel-chair, but Harry tears himself away, turns to Purkey.

HARRY: You want another take?

Purkey nods hopefully. Harry crosses to the wall switch beside the door.

SANDY (*taking a step toward him*): Harry –

Ignoring her, Harry turns on the overhead lights, joins Purkey at the window.

HARRY (*calling across the street*): What's your exposure?

108 EXT. WINDOW OF DETECTIVES' ROOM – EVENING

Max checks the camera.

MAX (*shouting back*): F-4.

109 INT. HARRY'S APARTMENT – NIGHT

Harry and Purkey are at the window.

HARRY (*to Max*): Stop it down to F-8. (*to Purkey*) You ready? (*Purkey nods; Harry calls out the window*) Roll it, Max.

He cocks his fist, throws another punch at Purkey's jaw. Purkey staggers back, lands in the wheel-chair.

HARRY (*toward the camera across the way*): So much for my bad hand.

He moves away from the window, stripping off his corset.

HARRY: Now let's see what a man with a broken back can do.

He tosses the corset in Willie's direction, grabs the curtain rod over the bedroom doorway, starts to chin himself. Purkey gets out of the wheel-chair, beaming, glances across the street, then hurries toward the hall door.

PURKEY (*to Harry*): Attaboy! Keep it up! (*he dashes out*)

Willie, watching Harry's performance with resignation, is pouring himself a glass of Kahlua.

SANDY (*frustrated*): Willie, why don't you *do* something!

WILLIE: Well, the *first* thing I'm going to do is cancel my reservation at the Persian Room. (*drinks*)

Harry swings forward on the bar, his feet brushing past Sandy's face. Sandy rears back, startled, then her hand flies to her right eye.

SANDY: My contact lens! I dropped it! (*to Willie*) Don't move!

She gets down on all fours, starts searching for the lens on the rug.

Harry swings backwards, lets go of the curtain rod, lands on the near bed.

HARRY (*toward camera*): Now, the most death-defying feat ever attempted by a man who just got out of a wheel-chair.

He bounces up into the air, does a somersault, continues to perform various other stunts on the bed, as if it were a trampoline.

110 EXT. WINDOW OF DETECTIVES' APARTMENT – NIGHT

Purkey hurries breathlessly into the room,

pushes Max away from the whirring camera, looks through the finder.

111 EXT. WINDOW OF HARRY'S APARTMENT – EVENING

Through the crossed hairs of the finder, Harry can be seen doing his trampoline act on the bed.

112 INT. HARRY'S APARTMENT – EVENING

Sandy is still crawling around on the floor, searching for the contact lens. Harry finishes his performance with a flourish, jumps off the bed, crosses to the window.

HARRY (*shouting across the street*): Did you get what you wanted?

Purkey makes a circle with his thumb and forefinger.

HARRY (*turning to Willie*): All right, genius – let's have the keys to my car.

WILLIE: You haven't got a car. They'll repossess it in the morning.

HARRY: They can have it in the morning. But right now I need it.

Willie tosses him the keys. Harry takes his duffel coat off the peg, starts putting it on.

HARRY (*to Sandy*): I don't want to find you here when I come back. And take that damn meatloaf with you!

He opens the hall door. Seeing Sandy's backside turned temptingly toward him, he can't resist. He boots her in the behind, and she goes sprawling forward on the rug.

HARRY (*to camera*): Nothing wrong with my leg, either.

He stalks out, slamming the door.

WILLIE: How did I ever marry into a family like this?

He moves to the window, looks out. Across the street, Max has started to remove the lens from the camera.

WILLIE (*shouting*): Wait a minute! I'm not through yet! Keep that camera rolling!

113 EXT. WINDOW OF DETECTIVES'
ROOM – EVENING
Max turns and looks questioningly at Purkey.
PURKEY (*magnanimously*): Go ahead. Let's see
him wriggle out of this one.
*Max screws the lens back on the camera, starts
the motor. Purkey puts on the earphones.*

114 INT. HARRY'S APARTMENT –
EVENING
*Willie reaches down into the radiator, fishes out
the mike, holds it up in front of him.*
WILLIE: This is William H. Gingrich, attorney
at law. I am both shocked and dismayed to
learn that my client has been deceiving me. But
there is no legal case against Mr. Hinkle –
(*produces the check*) – because no money has
changed hands. (*he tears the check up, tosses the
pieces out the window*) However, there *is* a legal
case against the firm of O'Brien, Thompson
and Kincaid. They have invaded the privacy
of my client – which is a violation of the Fourth
Amendment of the Constitution, and the
Federal Anti-Wiretapping Law of 1934. I am
therefore filing charges against these gentlemen
before the Ethical Practices Committee of the
American Bar Association. (*pacing, mike in
hand*) Furthermore, I am moving immediately
to revoke the license of one Chester Purkey,
private investigator.

115 EXT. DETECTIVES' WINDOW –
EVENING
*Max is busy photographing. The smug expression
on Purkey's face starts to congeal.*

116 INT. HARRY'S APARTMENT –
EVENING
*Willie is still pacing up and down in front of the
window.*
WILLIE (*into mike*): He has maligned a member
of a minority group, and I shall duly report this
fact to the Civil Rights Division of the Justice
Department, the Human Rights Commission
of the United Nations, the N-double A-CP,
CORE, the ACLU –
*Something crunches under his foot, and he
glances down.*
WILLIE (*to Sandy*): Oops! I think I found your
contact lens.

FADE.

16. The Final Score

117 INT. BOOM BOOM'S BOWLING
ALLEY – NIGHT
*The bar is empty, the lanes deserted – except for
Mr. Jackson, who is pushing a mop along one of
the alleys.*
*Harry, in his duffel coat, comes into the bar,
looks around. He spots Mr. Jackson through the
glass partition, hurries out toward him. He asks
a question, and Mr. Jackson points off. Harry
nods his thanks, heads for the rear door.*
DISSOLVE TO:

118 EXT. CLEVELAND MUNICIPAL
STADIUM – NIGHT
*In the vast, moonlit parking lot stands a lone
car – Boom Boom's white Cadillac.*
*The tan Mustang races into the lot, pulls up
alongside the Cadillac. Harry gets out, glances at
the empty car, proceeds toward the stadium
entrance.*

119 INT. STADIUM – NIGHT
*In the curved cement concourse under the stands,
a few cleaning women are at work, sweeping up
debris. The concession stands are shuttered, an
occasional light shines dimly overhead.*
*Harry comes through a turnstile, moves past the
cleaning women toward the dressing rooms, his
steps echoing in the stillness of the huge structure.*

INT. BROWNS' DRESSING ROOM – NIGHT

The walls are lined with open lockers – jam-packed with uniforms, helmets, shoes, toilet articles, etc. Above each locker is the name of a player. In the room are the equipment man, MAURY, and his assistant, both wearing Browns' T-shirts and caps. The assistant is sorting a pile of dirty uniforms. Maury is sitting on a trunk, screwing some new cleats into a football shoe with a pair of pliers. Next to him is a small stack of dollar bills. The assistant picks up a jersey from the pile, crumples it in his hand, holds it out to Maury.

MAURY (*after a moment's concentration*): Even!

The assistant unfolds the jersey – the number on the back is 27. The assistant smugly tosses the jersey into a laundry basket, takes a dollar from Maury's stack, shoves it in his pocket. He picks up another crumpled jersey, holds it out.

MAURY: Odd!

The assistant unfolds the jersey – it's number 38.

MAURY: This ain't my day.

As the assistant pockets another dollar, Harry comes in, looks around.

MAURY (*glancing up*): Yeah?

HARRY: Looking for Boom Boom Jackson.

MAURY: You're ten minutes late. (*points*) He just cleaned out his locker.

Harry steps up to the locker, which has the name JACKSON above it. It is empty except for a couple of wire hangers swaying on the rack.

MAURY: The team fighting to stay up there, and *this* has to happen. I would've believed it of some of the other guys – but Jackson – in a bar-room brawl – I don't know what got into him.

Harry stands there for a second, then turns and walks out. The assistant, resuming their game, picks up another crumpled jersey.

MAURY (*concentrating hard*): Even!

The assistant unfolds the jersey – it's 99. As he reaches cockily for another dollar, Maury grabs his hand.

MAURY: Wait a minute – we ain't got no ninety-nine!

He snatches the jersey from him, turns it right-side-up – it's actually number 66. He holds his hand out to the assistant, who reluctantly gives him a dollar bill from his pocket. Then he tosses the jersey in the assistant's face.

121 EXT. STANDS AND PLAYING FIELD – NIGHT

Harry comes out of a lighted tunnel, stops and looks around at the thousands of empty seats and the moonlit playing field.

The stadium isn't completely deserted. Sitting on the Browns' bench is a lonely figure in a camel's hair coat. It is Boom Boom, and on the bench beside him is a canvas bag. He has a book of matches in his left hand, and is holding a lighted match in his right. As the match goes out, he strikes another one, holds it up.

Harry, in the stands, spots the lighted match way off in the distance, starts toward it.

The match in Boom Boom's hand has burned down. As he strikes another one, he becomes aware of the sound of Harry's footsteps on the concrete steps. He looks off as Harry vaults over the railing of the stands, starts across the field toward the bench. As the figure gets closer, Boom Boom begins to realize that it is Harry. Harry arrives at the bench, stops in front of Boom Boom, who is just staring at him. A beat, then Harry indicates the canvas bag on the bench.

HARRY: Is this seat taken?

No answer from Boom Boom. Harry shoves the bag aside, seats himself beside Boom Boom. The match in Boom Boom's hand goes out, and he tosses it away.

HARRY: What's that with the matches?

BOOM BOOM (*not looking at him*): It's for a buddy of mine – Harry Hinkle – he's in a wheel-chair.

HARRY: Remember what you said in the hospital – what you'd do to anybody who called

your buddy a faker? Well, I say Harry Hinkle is a faker. (*no reaction from Boom Boom*) What are you waiting for? Go ahead – belt me.

BOOM BOOM (*quietly*): Why did you do it?

HARRY: For the money. What else?

BOOM BOOM: You're a liar.

HARRY: That's what I came to tell you.

BOOM BOOM: If it's for the money, how come you're out of that chair?

HARRY: Because I didn't like the set-up, and I didn't like the characters involved – especially me. So go ahead – do it. (*sticks his chin out, closes his eyes*)

BOOM BOOM: And put you back in that corset? Oh, no! I'm not going through *that* again.

There is a moment of silence. Then Harry's eyes fall on the canvas bag. It is unzipped, and crammed full of socks, underwear, toilet articles – and a football.

HARRY: I see you're all packed.

BOOM BOOM: Yeah. Shaving kit, three pairs of socks, and the football they gave me after the Baltimore game.

Harry takes the football out of the bag. Painted on it, in white letters, is the date: DECEMBER 27, 1964.

HARRY: Where are you going?

BOOM BOOM: I don't know. But somewhere between here and there, there's got to be a bar. (*rising*) Come on – I'll buy you a drink.

HARRY: Look, Boom Boom – they're going to make you sit out a couple of games – slap a big fine on you – but you'll be back.

BOOM BOOM: I don't care one way or the other. Because I'm through.

HARRY: Who says you're through?

BOOM BOOM: Eighty-three thousand people. When they boo you every time you come off the field – you begin to get the message.

HARRY: Sure, you were playing lousy. You had this mental block.

BOOM BOOM: I'm supposed to be a pro. Once you start to choke up – once you drop three punts in a row – you better look around for another line of work.

HARRY: Such as what?

BOOM BOOM: A guy my size and my weight – I can always go into the wrestling racket. I think I'd make a pretty good heavy. Call myself the Dark Angel.

HARRY: The Dark Angel?

BOOM BOOM (*picking up bag*): You coming?

HARRY (*glancing down at ball*): December 27th – You sure kept me busy that day, trying to follow you with the camera – forty-one yards, fifty-seven yards –

BOOM BOOM (*he doesn't want to hear about it*): So long, buddy. See you around.

He starts to walk across the field, toward the tunnel from which Harry emerged. Harry looks after him, unhappily. Then suddenly he rises, calls to Boom Boom.

HARRY: Hey! Boom Boom! You forgot something.

Boom Boom, who has now reached the goal-line, turns around. Harry punts the ball in his direction.

HARRY: Catch!

Boom Boom stands there, watching the ball come toward him. Then, at the last moment, he lets the bag slip from his hand, catches the ball, going into a half-crouch. He remains frozen in that position for a split-second.

HARRY (*yelling*): Go, man, go!

Out of reflex, Boom Boom starts to run with the ball, gathering momentum with every step. Harry angles across the field to intercept him. As Boom Boom comes thundering up, Harry lets go with a flying tackle, twining his arms around Boom Boom's legs. But Boom Boom stiff-arms him, brushing him off like a fly. He continues racing down the field till he crosses the opposite goal-line, touches the ball down, then glances back, winded but exhilarated. A look of alarm comes over his face.

Harry is sprawled in the middle of the field,

motionless.

Boom Boom rushes back toward him, the ball in one hand. He kneels beside Harry, lifts him up into a sitting position.

BOOM BOOM: Are you all right, buddy? Did I hurt you? (*slapping his face*) Buddy! Talk to me, buddy.

HARRY (*groggily*): Why doesn't one of you guys answer the phone?

BOOM BOOM: What phone?

HARRY: It's ringing.

BOOM BOOM: There's no phone here. (*his anxiety growing*) And how many of me do you see?

HARRY: Two.

BOOM BOOM: *Two?*

HARRY (*nods*): Boom Boom Jackson – and some nut who wants to call himself the Dark Angel! *A slow grin spreads across Boom Boom's face. Harry scrambles to his feet, grabs the football.*

HARRY: Come on, play ball!

They toss the ball back and forth, then Harry centers it. Boom Boom barks out a few signals, and Harry snaps the ball back, then starts down the field, running interference for him.

In the upper decks of the stands, three cleaning women stand leaning on their brooms, watching the game below.

On the field, Harry and Boom Boom are indulging in all sorts of razzle dazzle – criss-crossing, handing the ball off, lateralling to each other – and keeping up a constant stream of chatter. Finally Harry lofts a long pass to Boom Boom, who races across the goal-line and gathers it in.

HARRY (*throwing his hands up*): Touchdown!

Boom Boom toses the ball triumphantly into the air.

And that's the way the fortune cookie crumbles.

FADE OUT.

The End